Ontario Society of St. Vincent de Paul

Rules

Ontario Society of St. Vincent de Paul
Rules
ISBN/EAN: 9783744659833
Printed in Europe, USA, Canada, Australia, Japan
Cover: Foto ©ninafisch / pixelio.de

More available books at **www.hansebooks.com**

Society of St. Vincent of Paul.

HISTORICAL SKETCH.

At Paris, in the year 1833, in a house near the Public Schools, was a Literary Debating Society of students, whose sittings were conducted with all the animation that young minds usually impart to that kind of intellectual sparring, and likewise with all the serious interest which religious questions give to matters pertaining to them. Such questions frequently arose among the members ; all the great problems raised by their juvenile ardour, were based upon them. The students who adhered to the Catholic faith were drawn together by the necessity of openly professing its tenets and of defending them against their assailants; identity of faith, the power of religious sympathy, a sort of confraternity in arms, springing from the habit of fighting under the same banner, soon united their hearts and souls, and they became friends even before they had exchanged a word of friendship. They were then led to consider whether that faith which they were so happy to possess should not cement their union by some bond more consoling than controversy, which though necessary, was sometimes passionate, or offensive to piety ; they concluded that it was desirable to establish another association, exclusively Christian, over which charity alone should preside, and whose harmless object should be the worship of our Lord Jesus Christ in the persons of a few poor.

Such was the instinct of association from which sprang the first *Conference*; that denomination has been retained; it is adopted in Paris, for the literary meetings of young men; its meaning would be misunderstood if confined merely to the making of speeches on charity, or the discussing of methods for alleviating the condition of the poorer classes.

By placing itself from the first under the invocation of St. Vincent of Paul, in order to obtain through that great servant of God, a few sparks of the spirit of charity and faith which glowed within him, the Conference showed plainly that it was not by theoretical studies or declarations, but by deeds alone, according to the measure of their ability, that its members intended to follow at a distance the example of their blessed Patron.

The first meeting took place in May, 1833, it was composed of eight members only, under the Presidency of M. Bailly. In 1835 the number had increased to over 100. Another Conference was formed, and subsequently others, until the Society had spread over all the parishes of Paris and its vicinity. Many of the young men who composed these Conferences, returned at the close of their studies to their native Provinces; they naturally drew together and founded new Conferences after the model of those at Paris, and thus the Society found its way to every part of France.

The first Conference outside of France was very appropriately established at Rome, in 1842. In 1859 the Society was introduced into Spain, by a member from Paris, who wished to turn to advantage his visit to that country. 600 Conferences, with a membership of 10,000, who in one year, visited 15,000 families, and spent over £35,000, soon attested the happy result of his zealous benevolence. Meanwhile the Society had spread to England, Ireland, Scotland, Belgium, Holland, Prussia, Bavaria, Turkey, the Isles of Greece, in fact throughout and beyond Europe to Jerusalem, Bombay, Pondicherry, Mauritius, Isle Bourbon, (at Hong Kong is a Conference composed exclusively of Chinese), Cape of Good Hope, Buenos Ayres, Chili, Ecuador, and to come nearer home after circumnavigating the globe, to the West India Isles, Mexico and the United States of America. In view of this progress and at the solicitation of the General Council and of all the Superior Councils, His Holiness Pope Pius IX, was pleased to appoint one of the Sacred College, Cardinal Protector of the Society, which has thus a representative and an official promoter of its interests near the Holy See. Every one is familiar with the parable of the mustard seed; it has been verified in the extension of the Church, and whatever the Church approves should be co-extensive with her; the universal diffusion of the Society is thus readily accounted for.

In the United States the first conference was founded in 1846, at St. Louis, Missouri. After some delay the Society was organized in New

York City, and is now to be found actively employed at Boston, Philadelphia, Washington, New Orleans, and at almost every city or town of note in the length and breadth of the land.

In 1846 Dr. Joseph Painchaud, who had witnessed the good wrought by the members in Paris, founded at Quebec, the first Canadian Conference; almost simultaneously eight others were established in the same city. Montreal soon followed with five, which number has since been materially increased.

In November, 1850, the Conference of Our Lady was established at Toronto, by Mr. George Manly Muir, now President of the Superior Council, Quebec. This Conference may be considered the mother of those now existing throughout Ontario, most of them, if not all, owe their origin to the emigration as one may say, of members from this Conference or from others, which after its model, have since been formed in the city. The development of the Society in this Province, if slow, has been healthy; rapid progress is not always consistent with stability—the oak is a tree of slow growth, but when matured it is an oak.

In Ontario, the Society numbers as far as details have been furnished, the following Councils and Conferences :—

TORONTO.

Honorary President—The Most Reverend Archbishop of Toronto.

PARTICULAR COUNCIL.

(*Established* 19th December, 1853—*Organized* 26th February, 1854.)

President .... W. J. Macdonell.
Vice-President .... Charles Robertson.
Secretary .... J. J. Murphy.
Assistant Secretary .... Alex. Macdonell.
Treasurer .... Remy Elmsley.

Meets (temporarily) at the President's Rooms, 34 Church Street, on the second Wednesday of each month at 7.30 P.M.

CONFERENCE OF OUR LADY.

(*Organized* 10th November, 1850—*Aggregated* 6th January, 1851.

Spiritual Director..The Rev. Rector of St. Michael's.
President..........Patrick Hughes.
Vice-President .....James Britton.
Secretary ....John Monaghan.
Assistant Secretary..James Ryan.
Treasurer ....John Kelz.
Assistant Treasurer.Joseph Bondidier.

Meets in St. Michael's Palace every Sunday, immediately after High Mass.

CONFERENCE OF ST. PAUL.

(*Organized* 30th January, 1853—*Aggregated* 19th December, 1853.

Spiritual Director...The Rev. Parish Priest of St. Paul's.
President..........J. J. Mallon.
Vice-President......W. C. Barron.
Secretary ....Patrick Hynes.
Assistant Secretary..M. J. Hynes.
Treasurer ....Thomas Wright.

Meets every Sunday, at 2 P.M., in the House of Providence, Power Street.

CONFERENCE OF ST. MARY.*

(Organized as Conference of St. Patrick, 28th October, 1854—Aggregated 13th June, 1859.)

Spiritual Director..The Rev. Parish Priest of St. Mary's.
President..........Thomas Barry.
Vice-President......Patrick Cosgrave.
2nd Vice-President..Francis Rush.
Secretaries..........W. A. Lee, John Croake, and Wm. Looney.
Treasurer..........John Rogers.

Meets in the Chapel of St. Mary's Church, Bathurst Street, every Sunday, immediately after High Mass.

CONFERENCE OF ST. BASIL.

(Organized 7th January, 1857—Aggregated 31st October, 1859.)

Spiritual Director..The Rev. Parish Priest of St. Basil's.
President..........Richard Baigent.
Vice-President......James Fullerton.
Secretary...........Charles E. Stewart.
Treasurer..........J. J. Murphy.

Meets every Sunday, immediately after High Mass, in the Chapel of St. Basil's Church, Clover Hill.

CONFERENCE OF ST. PATRICK.

(Organized 20th April, 1862—Aggregated 29th February, 1864.)

Spiritual Director..The Rev. Parish Priest of St. Patrick's
President..........Martin Murphy.
Vice-President......R. S. Aymong.
Secretary..........Alexander Macdonell.
Treasurer..........Matthew Meyer.

Meets every Sunday, immediately after High Mass, in the Chapel of St. Patrick's Church, William Street.

COLLINGWOOD.

CONFERENCE OF ST. MARY.

(Organized 7th June, 1874.)

Spiritual Director..The Rev. Parish Priest.
President..........J. J. Long.
Vice-President......Patrick Boyle.

---

* St. Mary's Conference was originally known as the "Conference of St. Patrick," but on the erection of St. Patrick's Church, the latter title was, with the permission of the Superior Council of Paris, adopted by the Conference of St. Patrick's Parish.

Secretary..........A. J. O'Brien.
Treasurer..........James Guilfoyle.

Meets in the Church, every second Sunday, after Mass.

STAYNER.

CONFERENCE OF ST. PATRICK.

(Organized 15th October, 1876.)

Spiritual Director..Rev. M. O'Reilly.
President..........M. Gartlan.
Vice-President......Wm. Tobin.
Secretary..........Chas. O'Brien.
Treasurer..........T. Guilfoyle.

Meets every second Sunday, in St. Patrick's Church.

NEWMARKET.

CONFERENCE OF ST. MARY.

(Organized 3rd December, 1876.)

Spiritual Director..Rev. Father Harris.
President..........Edward Murphy.
Secretary..........James A. S. Kilman.
Assistant-Secretary..Thomas Gray.
Treasurer..........Patrick Harding.

Meets every second Sunday, after Mass.

ST. CATHARINES.

President..........Patrick Larkin.
Vice-President......Edward McArdle.
Treasurer..........Bernard King.
Secretary..........Joseph A. Woodruff.

KINGSTON.

CONFERENCE OF ST. MARY.

Honorary President.The Rt. Rev. The Bishop of Kingston.
Spiritual Director..Rev. Father Twohey.
President..........J. F. Swift.
Vice-President......Edward Hickey.
Secretary..........Pierce Browne.
Treasurer..........James McElhern.

BELLEVILLE.

Conference of Our Lady.

(Organized, as Conference of St. Michael, 26th February, 1871— Aggregated 16th September, 1872.)

Spiritual Director...V. Rev. J. Farrelly.
President..........David Holden.
1st Vice-President..John Doyle.
2nd Vice-President..David Brennan.
Secretary..........James Dunn.
Treasurer..........P. P. Lynch.
Assistant-Treasurer.Stephen Wade.

LINDSAY.

Conference of Our Lady.

(Organized April, 1872.—Aggregated 21st September, 1872.

Spiritual Director..Rev. M. Stafford.
President..........John Knowlson.
Vice-Presidents.....Wm. Duffus & C. L. Baker.
Secretary..........John W. Glascott.
Assistant-Secretary..John Pyne.
Treasurer..........John Berry.

Meets every Sunday, after Mass, 12.30, in St. Mary's Church.

PETERBOROUGH.

Conference of St. Peter.

(Organized 17th December, 1871.)

President................Alexander Vinette.
Vice-President..........James Dolan.
Secretary................Alfred McMurdy.
Corresponding Secretary..Daniel Sullivan.
Treasurer................Bryan Lynch.

Meets in Vestry, every Sunday, immediately after Mass.

HAMILTON.

Conference of Our Lady.

(Organized 30th July, 1865—Aggregated 18th June, 1866.)

Honorary President......The Rt. Rev. The Bishop of Hamilton.
Spiritual Director........Rev. M. Brennan.

President .... John Quinn.
Vice-President .... Henry Arland.
Secretary .... Francis Burdett.
Treasurer .... James M. Carthy.
Assistant Secretary &
  Patron of Schools } .. James Somerville.
Corresponding Secretary .. M. J. Forester.
Registrar .... Matthew McGloughin.
Recorder .... John Whalen.
Librarian .... Michael Brown.
Assistant Librarian ...... Henry Arland.
Keeper of Provisions ..... Michael Dake.
Assistant   do   ...... James Dwyer.
Keeper of Wardrobe ...... John Brown.
Trustees .... { P. S. McHenry.
                              Ed. Crofton.
                              Thomas Welsh.

Meets every Monday evening, at 7.30, in the basement of St. Mary's Church.

GUELPH.
Conference of Our Lady of Guelph.

Spiritual Director .. Rev. Ignatius Renaud, S.J.
President .... J. E. McElderry.
1st Vice-President .. W. S. Heffernan.
2nd Vice-President .. W. O'Connor.
Secretary .. .. Thomas Payne.
Assistant-Secretary. J. Dooley.
Treasurer .... Wm. Carroll.
Assistant-Treasurer. G. Searle.
Librarian .... F. Noonan.
Assistant Librarian. Thomas Howard.

Meets at 8 P.M. every Monday, in the Separate School House.

ARTHUR.

Spiritual Director .. Rev. J. Doherty.
President ... . Thomas Fogarty.
Vice-Presidents ..... Wm. McGill & Daniel Driscoll.
Secretary .... Edward J. Breen.
Treasurer .... Michael Fitzgerald.
Collector .... John McCarthy.
Librarian .... Thomas Murphy.

Meets every Monday, at 7.30 P. M., in the Separate School House.

LONDON.

PARTICULAR COUNCIL.

(Organized 16th December, 1877.)

Honorary President. The Rt. Rev. The Bishop of London.
Spiritual Director..Rev. Monsignor Bruyere.
President..........Richard Dynahan.
Vice-President......Anthony Henry.
Secretary..........Thomas Wright.
Treasurer..........Edward Goodrich.

CONFERENCE OF OUR LADY OF LONDON.

(Organized 15th December, 1859—Aggregated 21st September, 1863.)

Spiritual Director..Rt. Rev. J. Walsh.
President..........John Wright.
1st Vice-President..Philip Cook.
2nd Vice-President..Martin Gould.
Secretary..........John McLoughlan.
Treasurer..........Daniel Regan.

CONFERENCE OF THE SACRED HEART OF JESUS.

Spiritual Director..Rev. G. R. Northgraves.
President..........James Lacey.
Vice-President......Albert Curran.
Secretary..........Charles J. Quinn.
Treasurer..........Michael Mulkern.

STRATFORD.

CONFERENCE OF ST JOSEPH.

(Organized Easter, 1877.)

President..........James Corcoran.
Vice-President.......John O'Higgins.
Secretary..........M. C. Carey.
Treasurer..........J. Kneitt.

Meets in Temperance Hall, Ontario Street.

CHATHAM.

(Conference organized in 1873.)

President..........C. F. Sullivan.
Secretary..........James McGrath.
Treasurer..........Rev. Father Eugene, O. S. F.

Meets every Sunday, in the School house, after High Mass.

OTTAWA.

Particular Council.
(Organized May, 1865.)

Honorary President. The Rt. Rev. The Bishop of Ottawa.
President..........Moore A. Higgins.
Vice-President......R. Lapierre.
Secretary..........———
Treasurer..........C. Carleton.

Conference of Our Lady.
(Organized December 16th, 1860—Aggregated December 8th, 1862.)

President..........John O'Reilly.
Vice-Presidents......J. Sullivan & A. Harris.
Secretary..........George O'Keefe.
Treasurer..........N. McCaul.

Meets at 2 P.M., on Sundays.

Conference of Notre Dame.
(Organized 16th December, 1862—Aggregated September 21, 1863.)

President..........E. Millotte.
Vice-Presidents....R. Lapierre & H. Pinard.
Secretaries..........L. F. Casault & Z. Potvin.
Treasurers..........F. Rochon & Pierre Rivet.

Meets at 1.30 P.M., on Sundays.

Conference of St. Joseph.
(Organized 12th October, 1862—Aggregated 8th December, 1864.)

President..........Wm. Kehoe.
Vice-President......Eugene Tetu.
Secretary..........F. Desloges.
Treasurer..........C. Carleton,

Meets at 12 noon, on Sundays.

Conference of St. Patrick.
(Organized as Conference of St. Andrew, 6th July, 1862—Aggregated 21st September, 1863.)

President..........Charles McCarthy.
Vice-President......John Quain.
Secretary..........P. G. Leyden.
Treasurer..........D. Egan.

Meets at 12 noon, on Sundays.

Conference of St. Jean Baptiste.

President............C. P. Dorion
Vice-President.......J. B. Proulx.
Secretary..........G. Martineau.
Treasurer...........C. Gagné.

Conference of Ste. Anne.

President..........C. Robert.
Vice-Presidents....L. Z. Chabot & D Sauriol.
Secretaries..........D. Planchet & N. Sevigny.
Treasurers.........T. Labonté & E. Reulant.

Meets at 1 P.M., on Sundays.

PEMBROKE.

Conference of St. Patrick.

(Organized 8th February, 1863—Aggregated 4th July, 1864.)

President...........Michael Gorman.
1st Vice-President..G. Desjardins.
2nd Vice-President..G. Dixon.
Secretary.........A. J. Fortier.
Assistant-Secretary..Michael Shea.
Treasurer..........J. E. Whelan.

Meets every Sunday, at 3 P.M., in St. Patrick's Literary Association Hall.

Conferences, more or less developed, may exist at other places, but no definite information has been received from them.

It must be borne in mind that a Conference forms no part of the Society, as regards participation in the spiritual benefits accorded by the Church, until it has been *aggregated*; that is, until its claim to be considered such, has been duly proved before the General Council of Paris and formally admitted by that body. It is very possible that, for want of proper information, some of the Conferences above enumerated, have not yet undergone this ordeal; if so, application should be made at once, through the Superior

Council at Quebec, for the necessary recognition. —*See Page* 60.

The formation of a Superior Council in Toronto, for the governance of the Ontario Conferences, has for some time been in contemplation; this step, which will be taken when circumstances shall permit, will lessen the burden of the Superior Council of Quebec, and no doubt tend greatly to the local advancement of the Society.

The Society has been established for some years at Halifax and other points of importance in the Maritime Provinces, where its operations have been attended with beneficial results.

This, our fourth edition of the Rules, is published on the day of the coronation of Our Holy Father, Pope Leo XIII. May our brethren strive to merit at his hands a continuance of the favours so freely conferred upon our Society, by his illustrious predecessors, Gregory XVI, and Pius IX; and let us, according to our slender ability, endeavour to aid him in the discharge of the duties of his responsible position, by praying with the Church :

" *Dominus conservet eum, et vivificet eum, et beatum faciat eum in terra, et non tradat eum in animam inimicorum ejus.*"—AMEN.

TORONTO, March 3rd, 1878.

Order of Conference Meetings.

1. Prayer, by the President.
2. Pious Lecture, by a Member.
3. Reading Minutes of preceding Meeting.
4. Remarks on the same.
5. State of the Funds, by the Treasurer.
6. Candidates received as Members.
7. Candidates proposed for admission.
8. Poor adopted on Reports of Visitors.
9. Poor recommended; Visitors named.
10. Orders of the day; Suggestions; Remarks in general.
11. Collection made by a member.
12. Subject of Meditation, recommended by the President.
13. Prayer closing the meeting.
14. Distribution of Tickets to Visitors.

EXPLANATIONS
CONCERNING INDULGENCES.

I.

OF INDULGENCES IN GENERAL.

We are taught by Faith, that, after having obtained in the Sacrament of Penance the remission of sins committed after Baptism, as far as regards their guilt and the eternal punishment due to them, a temporal reparation generally remains to be made to Divine Justice; this is called atonement. The necessity of this atonement, after the sins have been forgiven, is recognized and admitted by all Catholic Doctors; and the works, by which we can atone to God, are prayer, alms, fasting, and submission to the Divine Will, in all the sufferings and afflictions of life. As these works of atonement, however, may be, for different causes, and are in fact, insufficient, the Church, which is infallible in her knowledge and the exercise of her spiritual powers, comes to the assistance of her children; and, in virtue of the authority vested in her by her Divine Founder, remits, in whole or in part, under certain conditions, however, which she takes care to prescribe and determine, the temporal punishment which has still to be undergone by them in this world or in the next.

This remission of temporal punishment due to sins which have already been pardoned, as far as regards their guilt and their eternal punishment, is granted by the Church, independently of the Sacrament of Penance, and is called *Indulgence.*

Indulgences do not relieve a person from the obligation of confessing his sins, of receiving absolution, and doing penance for them ; on the contrary, they pre-suppose all these things, and merely supply, by the application which the Church makes in our favour of the super-abundaant atonements of Jesus Christ, the Blessed Virgin and the Saints, the insufficiency of the satisfaction that we might offer ourselves.

The infinite atonement of the Son of God and the atonements of the Blessed Virgin, and of many Saints, who, during their lives, more than satisfied for their sins, actually form, as declared by Pope Clement VI., a real treasure, into which flow continually new spiritual riches, of which the Church has been appointed by Divine authority the sole and sovereign dispenser.

It is from this treasure that the Church draws the *Indulgences* granted by her to the faithful, to supply or complete the atonement they owe to Divine Justice.

Indulgences are *plenary* or *partial.*—They are *plenary* when they remit the whole of the temporal punishment due to sin, the guilt of which must, however, have been previously wiped out by the Sacrament of Penance. They are *partial* when they remit a portion only of the temporal punishment due to sin ; for instance, seven years and seven times forty days, more or less.

In thus granting a specific number of days, weeks, or years of indulgence, the Church does not pretend to shorten for a corresponding period the sufferings of purgatory ; she merely intends remitting a portion of temporal pain equal to that which would have been remitted by the same number of days, weeks, or years of the canonical penance which was formerly prescribed by the *Penitential Canons.*

Plenary or *partial* Indulgences may be applied to the souls in purgatory, only, however, when the Briefs or Rescripts. by which they are granted, permit and authorize this application. The Church does not apply Indulgences directly to the dead, for over them she can have no more jurisdiction ; it is therefore to the living Faithful that these Indulgences are granted. They accomplish the works imposed and offer to God, for the dead, by way of *suffrage*, the satisfactory value of the Indulgence, conjuring Him to accept it for the total or partial remission of the temporal punishment the departed souls may have yet to expiate.

All Catholic Doctors affirm that these Indulgences are accepted by God and are beneficial to the souls in purgatory. But it is impossible to determine in what degree and to what extent God applies them to the souls for whose relief they are intended. This application depends, as regards the extent of its effects, upon the

Sovereign Will of God, who has not in this case, as in the case of Indulgences to the living, to ratify a sentence of His Church.

II.

Conditions required to gain the Indulgences.

The conditions prescribed to gain the Indulgences have reference, either to the dispositions of the faithful, or to the works enjoined :—

On the part of the faithful, two dispositions are required, *the state of Grace* and *the intention* to gain the Indulgences. 1st. That a person in the state of mortal sin cannot gain an Indulgence admits not of a doubt. Liable to everlasting punishment so long as he remains in that state, he cannot claim the remission of temporal punishment due to sins that have neither been confessed nor forgiven. With regard to the attachment to venial sin, it does not prevent the obtaining of the Indulgences, which, in this case, may be applied to other sins already remitted. However, these Indulgences cannot be plenary, because the temporal punishment due to a sin, though it were venial, cannot be remitted, unless the sin itself has been forgiven, which cannot take place as long as an affection for that sin shall continue. 2ndly. The intention required to gain the Indulgence may be formed in the morning, and applied to all good works to be performed in the course of that day, and to which Indulgences are attached. 3rd. As regards the works to be done and the manner of performing them, the terms of the Briefs or Rescripts that grant the Indulgences must be strictly adhered to.

INDULGENCES,

GRANTED BY THE BRIEFS OF THE SOVEREIGN PONTIFFS GREGORY XVI AND PIUS IX, DATED JAN. 10, AND AUG. 12, 1845; MARCH 18, 1853; MARCH 28, 1854; AND SEPTEMBER 13TH, 1859, TO THE SOCIETY OF ST. VINCENT DE PAUL; TO THE BENEFACTORS OF THE SOCIETY, AND TO THE POOR ASSISTED BY IT.

SEC. I.

INDULGENCES GRANTED TO THE MEMBERS OF THE SOCIETY.

1. *A Plenary Indulgence* once each month to the Members of the General Council, and of the Particular Council of Paris, and of any other city, who, besides complying with the usual conditions, shall have been present at all, or three out of the four meetings of their Council held during the month.

2. *A Plenary Indulgence* once each month to all *Active* Members, on the usual conditions, and provided they shall have been present at all, or at three out of the four, Conference Meetings held during the month. This Indulgence can also be gained by the Members of Councils who

may already have gained the above-mentioned Indulgence.

3. *A Plenary Indulgence* on the day of reception as an Aspirant Member, an Ordinary Member, or Member of any Particular Council, or of the General Council, the usual conditions having been complied with.

4. *A Plenary Indulgence* to both *Active and Honorary* Members, who, (i) on the Festival of the Immaculate Conception of the Blessed Virgin Mary, or on the Sunday within the octave, or, if it is transferred, on the day (*a*) on which it is celebrated—(ii) on the Feast of St. Vincent de Paul, and the seven days immediately following, once only during this space of eight days—(iii) on the second Sunday after Easter, and (iv) on the First Sunday in Lent, (*b*) being truly penitent, and having confessed their sins, shall receive the Holy Sacrament at the Mass which, on the aforesaid days, is celebrated for the Society, and shall have been present at the General Meeting which is held on those occasions.

5. *A Plenary Indulgence* at the hour of death to *all Members* of this Society, who, being truly penitent, and confessing their sins, or, should circumstances prevent their doing this, being at

---

(*a*) By the Brief of Sept. 13th, 1859, beginning ; "*Renunciandum curavit*," the Indulgence annexed to the Festival of the Immaculate Conception may be gained on the Sunday within the Octave (*b*) and that heretofore granted on the first Monday in Lent is transferred to the previous day. By the same Brief, all the Indulgences mentioned in this paragraph can be gained even if the Mass, at which the Members *assist together*, be not offered for the Society.

least contrite, shall with their lips, or, if unable to do so, in their hearts, devoutly invoke the *holy name of Jesus*, and shall, with a patient and ready mind, accept death from the hand of the Lord as a penalty for sin.

6. *An Indulgence of Seven Years and as many times Forty Days*, as often as an *Active* Member shall, with a contrite heart, visit any Conference or poor family, or the schools or workshops of the poor, or perform any other good work in accordance with the spirit of the Society, or shall assist at the Holy Sacrifice of the Mass when celebrated for the soul of any member, or shall follow the bodies of the poor to ecclesiastical interment.

The above Indulgences extend to Members who live in places where as yet no Conference exists, provided they perform, as far as they can, the customary works, and fulfil the other prescribed conditions.

7. *A Plenary Indulgence* to *all Members* who have attended devoutly each day to the Spiritual Exercises which take place for the Members collectively, and who, being truly penitent, and having confessed, shall receive the Holy Communion at the Mass on the last of these days, and offer prayers for the concord of Christian princes, the uprooting of heresies, and the exaltation of our Holy Mother the Church.

8. *An Indulgence of one hundred days* to the Members who, contrite of heart, shall have fulfilled only a part of the Spiritual Exercises, and shall have prayed as above.

N.B.—All the above Indulgences may be applied by way of suffrage to the souls in purgatory.

SEC. II.

INDULGENCES GRANTED TO THE BENEFACTORS.

1. *A Plenary Indulgence* once a month to all and every one of the faithful, *whether men or women*, who shall regularly give to the General Council some fixed alms, provided they be truly penitent, confess their sins, and receive the Holy Communion.

2. *An Indulgence of Seven Years and as many times Forty Days*, once each month to all the faithful, *whether men or women*, who shall regularly transmit some fixed alms to the Particular Councils established by the General Council for towns or provinces.

3. *An Indulgence of One Year*, obtainable, likewise, once each month by such of the faithful, *men or women*, who shall, in writing or otherwise, engage to give regularly some fixed alms to Conferences approved by the General Council, or by Particular Councils empowered to approve by the General Council.

4. *An Indulgence of Seven Years and as many times Forty Days*, to all the faithful, *whether men or women*, obtainable once each month, on the days when they solicit and collect contributions in aid of the Councils, whether General or Particular.

5. *A Plenary Indulgence* at the hour of death to *all benefactors* of the Society, who, being truly

penitent, and confessing their sins, or should circumstances prevent their doing this, being at least contrite, shall, with their lips, or, if unable so to do, in their hearts, devoutly invoke *the holy name of Jesus,* and shall, with a patient and ready mind, accept death from the hand of the Lord as a penalty for sin.

The Brief of the 13th of September, 1859, beginning : " *Renunciandum curavit,*" grants to each and every member of the faithful *connected in any way* with this Society, *or Benefactors* to the same, an Indulgence of Three Hundred Days as often as they shall, with a contrite heart, recite in any language the peculiar prayer of the Society, which begins " We give thee thanks," &c. (*See Page* 102.)

SECTION III.

INDULGENCES GRANTED TO THE POOR ASSISTED BY THE SOCIETY.

The same Brief grants a Plenary Indulgence on Christmas day, on the feast of St. Joseph, and on the closing day of the Annual Retreat, to all persons, men or women, to whom the Society of St. Vincent de Paul gives assistance, provided that, being truly contrite and having gone to confession and received the Holy Communion, they shall have visited devoutly any church or public oratory, and have prayed there for concord amongst Christian princes, the extirpation of heresy, and the exaltation of our Holy Mother the Church. On the two first mentioned feasts, the visit to the church should take place after the first vespers of the feast, and on the closing day of the Retreat any time between sunrise and sunset.

The same Brief grants an Indulgence of One Hundred Days to all those who are assisted by the Society, provided they shall have recited with contrite hearts, either alone or in their families, the Lord's Prayer and the Angelical Salutation, adding in any language the following invocations:

"Queen, conceived without original sin, pray for us."

"St. Vincent de Paul pray for us."

These Indulgences are applicable to the souls in Purgatory.

Countersigned, ✝PAUL CULLEN,
Archbishop,

Dublin, November 15th, 1860.

INTRODUCTION.

Society of St. Vincent of Paul.

IMPORTANT POINTS TO BE KEPT IN VIEW BY ALL MEMBERS OF THE SOCIETY.

1. Vigilant Attention, in the Choice of Members.

Nothing is more injurious to a Conference, than an *inconsiderate* increase of the number of its members. Far better to be few, provided they be exact in complying with all required duties. If, in effect, a Conference admit individuals who do not fulfil the essential duties prescribed by the Church, more especially the indispensable precept of Paschal Communion, it runs great risk of soon degenerating into a purely human work of benevolence, thereby losing sight of the spiritual good of its poor. Besides this primary and necessary qualification, a candidate for admission should have a sincere esteem for the Society, be disposed to sacrifice *self*, to love the poor, and be of a conciliatory and charitable character.

2. *Assiduity in Visiting the Poor.*

This work is the distinctive characteristic of the Society, according best with its wants, and best adapted to revive the zeal of its members. By accustoming ourselves to sit by the hearths of the poor, to see for ourselves their physical and moral destitution, we learn how to love them and relieve their wants. Moreover, this work is easy ; it does not demand a long apprenticeship, or exact time not at the disposal of every one. The Conferences should, above all things, strictly practise these *domiciliary visits*, in the Christian spirit of their beloved Patron, St. Vincent of Paul. When, in attending the poor, we feel convinced that we visit Jesus Christ, this duty will always be discharged with love and fidelity.

3. *Punctual Attendance at the Meetings, and Cordiality among the Members.*

These two points are closely connected, and cannot be safely disregarded. Without punctuality, the meetings languish, members are disheartened, collections diminish, and it becomes impossible to undertake many useful works, which, otherwise, could be easily accomplished. Again, without cordiality, the meetings become tiresome and uninteresting ; attended perhaps as *matter of duty ;* but not with that *pleasure* which members of flourishing Conferences experience on being brought together. A Conference never fails in its objects, by being animated by decent and Christian cheerfulness ; on the contrary, many have suffered for want of that mutual kindliness among their members which is a sign of fraternal union.

4. Frequent Intercourse with other Conferences.

The members of each Conference should be fully aware that they form not so much parts of a single Conference, *as of the whole Society*. They should, therefore, highly esteem their relation with neighbouring Conferences ; with the particular or Central Council upon which they mutually depend ; and finally, with the General Council—the centre of the whole Society. In the spirit of union has hitherto lain the strength of the Conferences ; and in proportion as that spirit continues will be their future progress.

5. Observance of the Feasts and General Meetings.

By the Rules of the Society, General Meetings should be held at least four times a year ; namely, on the 8th December, first Monday in Lent, second Sunday after Easter, and 19th July. We must not forget that our Society is intended, *primarily*, for the spiritual improvement of its members ; they should *practice* what they wish to teach others. It is, therefore, highly desirable that all attend the General Meetings on the days indicated, and comply with the other conditions required for gaining the Plenary Indulgences granted for those occasions. By *first amending ourselves* we may piously hope that God will bless our endeavours for the amendment of our neighbours.

6. Deferential and Respectful Bearing toward the Clergy.

Essentially Catholic, our Society should always maintain as a singular honour, a close connection with the Parochial Clergy and Bishop of the Diocese. Its intimate union with the Church, (of which the blessing of the Episcopate and high approval of the Sovereign Pontiff are precious guarantees) is, for the Society of St. Vincent of Paul, as for all Catholic works, an indispensable condition of stability, and the most necessary of all duties.

7. Perseverance and Resignation in Difficulties—Necessity of Humility.

The exercise of charity is sometimes impeded by obstacles and crosses; Conferences equally with other organizations, are not exempt therefrom. In such circumstances, the members must not be dejected ; but, on the contrary, consider them as signs of the Divine blessing. If faithful to this counsel, they endeavour always patiently to support contradictions, avoid strife and contention, and wait their justification from time and Almighty God, their forbearance will receive a most certain recompense. But, should Heaven deign to bless their labours, by granting evident success, this favour must always be placed beneath the powerful safe-guard of humility. Our *confreres* should habitually remember, that, when they shall have done whatever has been enjoined, they are, after all, but " unprofitable servants." ST. LUKE, xvii, 10.

RULES

OF THE

Society of St. Vincent of Paul,

TORONTO.

Extracted from the Regulations Published at Paris in December, 1835.

Here at last is the beginning of that written organization which was the object of our wishes. It has long been delayed, for some years have passed since our little association was commenced. But before receiving a definite form of existence, was it not necessary to ascertain whether or no God willed it to live? Was it not necessary that it should have a settled basis, that the will of Heaven in its regard should be known, that we might judge of what it could do by what had been done, before adopting rules and prescribing duties? Now we have only had, as it were, to transfer into regulations, practices that have already been followed and cherished. This is a sure guarantee that our regulations will be universally well received and will not fall into oblivion.

Our little congregation was at first styled the

Conference of Charity of St. Vincent of Paul. It was so called because under this name it commenced, and in order that the circumstances of its origin, which no one in particular can refer to himself might not be forgotten. It occurred to some young men, while defending religious dogmas in the stormy debates of literary societies, that speaking was not sufficient, but that action also was necessary; hence the works of charity to which they devoted themselves; hence the *Conference of Charity.*

Having greatly increased in numbers and being obliged to divide into sections, several of us, again, wishing to re-unite in other cities where our future lot was cast, each section, all of which are comprised under the common denomination of *The Society of St. Vincent of Paul*, continued to be called a *Conference.*

We shall ever avoid giving our association the name of any of its members, whatever services he may be considered to have rendered, or of any of the places in which it may hold its meetings, lest we should accustom ourselves to look upon it as the work of man; works of Christian charity belong to God alone, the author of all good.

A movement of Christian piety first brought us together; therefore we seek our rules of conduct in the spirit of religion, in the examples and precepts of Our Lord, in the teachings of the Church, and in the Lives of the Saints; therefore we have placed ourselves under the patronage of the Blessed Virgin and St. Vincent of Paul, to whom we pay particular honour, and in whose footsteps we endeavour to walk.

Christ began by practising what he was afterwards to teach mankind : *cœpit facere et docere :* (Acts, i, 1.) our desire is to imitate this Divine Model, as far as our weakness will permit.

The object, aim, and end of this Society is : 1st, to encourage its members, by example and counsel, in the practice of a Christian life. 2nd, to visit the poor at their dwellings ; to carry them succour in kind,—to afford them also religious consolation, remembering these words of our Master, "*Not in bread alone doth man live, but in every word that proceedeth from the mouth of God,*" (Deut. viii. 3 ; Matt. iv. 4). 3rd. To apply ourselves according to our abilities and the time we can spare, to the elementary and Christian instruction of poor children, whether free or imprisoned, seeing that what we do for the least among our brethren, Jesus Christ has promised he will accept as done to Himself. 4th, to distribute moral and religious books. 5th, to be willing to undertake any other sort of charitable work to which our resources may be adequate, and which does not oppose the chief end of the Society.

The Society is composed of *active, aspirant* and *honorary* members. The members of this latter class assist the former by their efforts and by their influence ; by their offerings and by their prayers, they supply the absence of that actual co-operation which their ordinary engagements will not permit them to undertake.

The Society should endeavour to attain and practise every virtue; there are, however, some virtues which are more essentially necessary to its members, for the due discharge of the charitable duties to which they devote themselves. Among these are, self-denial, Christian prudence, the active love of our neighbour, zeal for the salvation of souls, meekness in heart and word, and above all, the spirit of fraternal charity. Its members should therefore meditate on those maxims of the Gospel which recommend these virtues, and make them the rule of their lives. For this purpose these maxims are here detailed, and a development given to them applicable to the objects of our Institution.

1. By *self-denial* we should understand the surrendering of our own opinion, without which surrender no association is durable. The man who is in love with his own ideas will disdain the opinion of others; which disdain, far from uniting, will engender division. We should therefore willingly acquiesce in the judgment of others, and should not feel annoyed if our own propositions be not accepted by them. Our mutual good will should proceed from the heart, and should be without bounds. We ought equally to avoid all spirit of contention with the poor, and must not consider ourselves offended, if they yield not implicitly to our advice; we should not attempt to make them receive it as from authority and by command, but, contenting ourselves with proposing what is good, and zealously exhorting to its practice, leave the result entirely in the hands of Almighty God.

2. Among the poor there are some who have the happiness to be devout Christians; others are indifferent, and some perhaps impious. We ought not to repulse them, even in this latter case; but our language should be applicable to the dispositions of those whom we address; remembering that Jesus Christ recommended his disciples to unite the wisdom of the serpent to the simplicity of the dove. Generosity opens the heart to confidence, and charitable gifts prepare the way for spiritual benefits. St. Vincent of Paul often recommended his followers not to try the latter, until the former had been freely bestowed.

3. *Love of our neighbour and a zeal for the salvation of souls.*—This is the essence of the Society. He who is not animated by this twofold sentiment, which with the Christian forms but one feeling, should not become a member. We must never murmur at the labours, the fatigues, nor even at the repulses to which the exercise of charity may subject us. We expose ourselves to all these things, in associating for the service of our neighbour. Neither should we regret the pecuniary sacrifices that we may make to our Institution; on the contrary, we should esteem ourselves happy in offering anything to Jesus Christ in the persons of the poor, and in being able to carry any relief to his suffering members. We should make these sacrifices with an entire absence of personal feeling, and not conceive that the poor whom we have adopted ought to be more privileged than those adopted

by others, merely because we may have contributed to the common fund a larger portion than they.

4. Our Divine Model was meek and humble of heart; "*Learn of me, because I am meek and humble of heart,*" (Matt. xi 29); and our patron, St. Vincent of Paul, prized nothing so highly as meekness and humility, which are inseparable. To each other we should be kind and obliging, and we should adopt the same sentiments toward the poor whom we visit. We can have no power over the mind, except through meekness; all blessings also are promised to those who use this method. "*Blessed are the meek for they shall possess the land.*" (Matt. v, 4.) The spirit of humility and meekness is particularly necessary in giving advice, and in exhorting others to fly from evil, and to practice virtue. Without gentleness, zeal for the salvation of souls is like a ship without sails.

5. By the spirit of brotherly love our Society will become dear to its members, and edifying to others. Faithful to the maxims of Our Divine Master and of His beloved disciple, let us love one another. Let our brotherly affection be constant, now and ever, far and near, from one Conference to another, from town to town, from clime to clime. This brotherly love will enable us to bear with each other's failings; we shall never think ill of a brother without regret, and only when we cannot longer refuse to acknowledge the evidence of facts; even then (in order to conform ourselves to the will of Him who has confided

to each one the care of his neighbour, (Eccles. xvii 12), in a spirit of charity, and with all the heartfelt effusion of the most devoted friendship for our fallen or falling brother, we will counsel him ourselves, or cause advice to be conveyed to him. We will endeavour to strengthen him in virtue, or raise him from his fall. If any member of the Society should become ill, his brethren will visit him; will tend him, if necessary; will soften and assuage the tediousness of his slow recovery; or if his malady be dangerous, they will see that the consolations which religion affords be his, and that the Holy Sacraments be administered to him. In a word, the troubles and joys of one shall be shared by all, in accordance with the advice of the apostle, who has desired us to weep with those who weep, and rejoice with those who rejoice.

The unity of the Society of St. Vincent of Paul should be cited as a model of Christian friendship; of a friendship carried beyond the grave; for in our prayers before the Almighty we shall remember those of our brethren who have gone before us.

This sentiment of fraternal charity, this union of hearts and souls, will endear to each of us our little Society. We shall bless it for the good, however trivial, it enables us to perform; we shall love our society with tenderness, and even with a greater affection than any other association of the kind, not from pride, or because of its excellence, but as affectionate children would love a tender, though poor and deformed mother, more than all other women, however they might excel by their riches or their talents.

A few other Considerations on the foregoing Maxims.

One of the vices most opposed to charity and Christian humility is envy. We should be vigilant on this point, not only among ourselves, but with respect to other Societies whose object, like our own, is the solace and relief of our neighbour. We should ardently desire, and behold with pleasure, their prosperity, and the good they accomplish; we should rejoice if fresh brethren join us, if existing societies unite themselves to ours, since greater good may spring from the union; we should behold without jealousy our Christian friends devoting themselves to other good works, and other Societies doing God's work in their own manner and independently of us. We should have but one desire,—that of seeing all engaged in doing good, and in consoling those who suffer; not considering our work the best, but loving it the most.

The same spirit should ever induce us individually to wish that the offices of the Society should be confided to others, rather than to ourselves.

We should always remember that we are only laics, and for the most part young men, without any mission to teach others; we should therefore show the utmost deference to good counsel which may be given to us by the Society and its heads; and we must above all, observe and follow with docility the directions which our ecclesiastical superiors may think fit to give us. St. Vincent of Paul wished his disciples not to undertake any good work, without having first secured the assent, and received the benediction of the local pastors. We should likewise, to a certain degree, extend this deference to the Sisters of Charity, and even to laymen who may have offices of charity to perform towards those whom we also desire to succour; considering it an honour to be the least among our brethren, and wishing to be no more than the servants and instruments of others in the assistance rendered to the poor. Lastly among ourselves the younger should defer to the elder, and newly admitted members to those who are of longer standing.

We are the dispensers of the gifts of God, who, is the common Father of mankind, and makes His sun to shine upon all. Our love of our neighbour must then be without respect of persons. The title of the poor to our commiseration is their poverty itself. Jesus Christ came to redeem and save all men; Greeks as well as Jews, barbarians as well as Romans. We should not discriminate any more than He did, between those who are victims of suffering and misery. Nevertheless, St. Paul recommends Christians to assist, in the *first* place their brethren in the faith (Galatians, 6, 10.) We, should therefore, manifest a special interest for those poor who are punctual in the observance of their religious duties, and who honour the title of Christian by the practice of the virtues which religion inculcates.

The spirit of charity, as well as Christian prudence, will ever induce us to banish from our meetings all political discussion. St. Vincent of Paul wonld not allow his ecclesiastics to converse upon differences which create war among princes, or to discuss motives of rivalry which sometimes estrange nations. It is still more essentially necessary that those who wish to be of one mind and to exercise the ministry of charity, should discard all political questions which bring parties into conflict; and refrain from those irritating subjects which so often agitate society. Our Society is all charity — politics are foreign to its purpose.

The choice of new members is of the utmost importance, in order to maintain effectually that unity of sentiment and to cement that Christian friendship which form the foundation and the charm of our Society. Previously therefore, to the enrolment of any friend in our ranks, we should carefully enquire whether he be calculated to draw closer those ties which bind us to each other; whether the amenity of his disposition and his Christian mildness would enhance the value of that relief which he may be commissioned to afford to the wretched; whether the firmness of his disposition authorizes us to hope that he will persevere in carrying out his generous resolutions; and whether he is in a condition to contribute to the funds of the Institution. Nothing could be more disastrous than that it should for an instant be supposed that the alms entrusted to the Sons of St. Vincent of Paul had been applied to the personal wants of any one of their members. Another essential rule, upon the observance of which the future prospects of the Society mainly depend, and which the Conferences have rigorously followed, is to admit such persons only as are sincerely attached to the Catholic Faith, not merely by habit, but heartily and with an entire conviction; persons in a word, who observe the commandments of God and of the Church. It is only by undeviating rectitude of life, and constancy in the performance of those acts of charity to which we have devoted ourselves, that our confreres can inspire confidence and become efficient in promoting the charitable aim of the Society.

Another point no less worthy of our consideration is the discretion which should accompany our zeal for the salvation of souls. The human heart is not always in a fit state to receive Christian teaching. We must wait with patience the hour which God has appointed; as He is patient, so must we be. It is possible that weeks may pass without our being able to inculcate with effect a single maxim of morals or religion. We must not be importunate upon this point. We are not commissioned to perform good which it is out of our power to effect. Neither should we be discouraged at the apparent fruitlessness of our endeavours. Perhaps the Almighty wills not that we ourselves should witness the happy end which may result from our efforts and our sacrifices. Our charity would be less meritorious and might dispose us to vain glory if we beheld it always successful.

The first work of the Society of St. Vincent of Paul, that which most of all appears essential to it, is the visit of the poor at their abodes.— We can never know so well what the unfortunate suffer, as when we go to their dwellings and become witnesses of all their wants and of all their sufferings. The sight of so many privations is the best preservative against the abuse of riches—Can we indulge in every fancy, and take a pleasure in luxuries, when we see near us so many persons in need of the necessaries of life? This spectacle is salutary, especially for a young man just entering the world—in the midst of the giddiness produced by parties and pleasures, the visit to a poor family will arrest him more forcibly on the slippery declivity down which he is borne, than could all the counsels of wisdom. He is compelled to reflect; he sees life as it is; illusions vanish and are succeeded by serious and useful thoughts.

Again, when we take to the poor a little bread to appease their hunger, a few garments to cover their nakedness, we often receive in exchange, graces and instructions far more precious; we learn patience and resignation in the midst of sufferings; we gain peace and serenity of soul. It is Jesus Christ Himself whom we visit, when we visit the poor; we go to a faithful friend by whom we are always well received; we return with joy and contentment of heart; many of our confreres have declared that they have derived ineffable spiritual benefit from visiting the poor confided to their care.

We repeat, the visit of the poor at their dismal abodes is the distinctive character of the Society of St. Vincent of Paul; the Council of Paris has even exhorted the Presidents of the Conferences of that city to visit in person, occasionally, all the families adopted by their respective Conferences, to enable them to become better acquainted with their wants, and to assure themselves that the visits are regularly made.

This visit of the poor, so useful to all who practice it, so proper to entertain in them the spirit of charity by a knowledge of the details of suffering, may under another aspect and with regard to the poor themselves, be viewed as the foundation of all the other works of the Society. It is the first step to be made in the career of Charity. Let us then go courageously to those infectious dens where poverty is too often condemned to dwell; let us enter into conversation with the poor; a few kind words will gain their confidence, which moreover is soon acquired by him who goes to relieve and to console; we shall learn all their sufferings, all their wishes; we shall give them advice founded on a knowledge of facts; we shall cause their children to go to good schools, or be placed in apprenticeship, and withdrawn from idling in the streets. By thus having forethought for the poor, who seldom have forethought for themselves, we will, in a manner, be their Providence, and prepare for them better days.

Christian prudence should ever accompany our mission to the poor. Unfortunately, especially in large towns, the poor often conceal their means of subsistence, and thus draw to themselves that sympathy and those alms which should be shared by others. Without therefore, entertaining suspicions injurious to the interests of the poor, we should use great circumspection in administering relief. It is not wise to rely too implicitly upon their first statements. It will therefore be a duty to ascertain their real condition from the clergy or from persons most likely to afford us information upon the subject. If we wish to become their true benefactors we should represent to them how precarious are the means of charity which we have at our disposal, and how necessary it will be for them to endeavour to earn their own subsistence. In so doing we ought to assist them and point out the means of obtaining employment. If they be ill and unable to work we should aid them in obtaining admission into those establishments for which they may be eligible.

Let us remember likewise, that we must never be ashamed to give trivial alms. That which is small in the estimation of the rich is great in the eyes of the poor who possess nothing. Our ordinary resources must depend upon the voluntary offerings of each of us, assisted by the charitable contributions of our friends. If these resources do not allow us to bestow large alms, our tender interest for the poor, our very manner towards them, will add to our gifts a value which of themselves they do not possess.

The house of the poor is the point of departure for charitable thoughts; it is there we put to profit and combine the works already projected by the piety of the faithful; it is there we imagine new modes of relieving new wants, and of preventing the recurrence of the evils which afflict them.

Ah! what a consolation for a young man, if all his life he can keep in-view a family which he has assisted, which he has withdrawn from misery, and perhaps reclaimed from the grossest vices! Who can tell all the graces that God will pour on him, as a reward of the generous action that marked the commencement of his career.

The members of some Conferences, have caused the poor to come to their own houses to receive relief and advice, instead of going themselves to the abodes of the poor. This is less contrary to our Institution than causing assistance to be taken to the poor by servants; this last mode cannot be too strongly blamed; nothing would tend more radically to destroy the spirit of the Society; the abnse, however, has as yet, revealed itself by but one isolated act, and loud were our complaints thereupon. We gave the cry of alarm, as if the enemy had been at our door; we hope that this cry is still heard by all, and that we shall be sufficiently watchful over one another, to prevent the recurrence of a similar misfortune.

As regards making the poor come to our houses, we blame that course likewise. The foundation, the essence of our work, is visiting the poor in their dismal abodes ; we must see them in all their rags, in all their neglect, in the inconveniences of their misery, in their improvidence, in their discouragement. This sight is at once an instruction, and a motive to engage us to devote ourselves to their relief. If they come to us instead, the desired result will not be obtained. Who does not feel that a spontaneous charitable visit to an indigent family will ensure to the visitor a moral ascendency over that family, not to be derived from an interview which one of its members might come to seek from interested motives ? But let us here elevate our thoughts higher ; the poor are the friends of Jesus Chrst ; they are His members ; they are Himself ; Jesus Christ holds as done to Himself what we do for each of them ; St. Vincent of Paul wished that, when we spoke to the poor, when we gave them alms, we should represent to ourselves and be convinced that we spoke to Jesus Christ himself, that we assisted the Divine Saviour in person. Who among us does not envy the happiness of the Shepherds of Bethlehem ? This happiness we share, when we visit with faith the poor at their dwellings, in their humble mangers, nay, we may even say, in their stables. Like those happy shepherds, let us be anxious to perform this pious work ; let us hasten to the cellars, to the garrets, to every place where the Divine Infant suffers in the persons of the poor; let us approach these miserable haunts with respect, veneration, and love; let us not abandon to others so high a privilege. A great favour was granted to a few humble shepherds on the very night of the birth of our Lord; a great favour also is conferred upon the members of the Society of St. Vincent of Paul, in being called to the honour, and to the blessing of visiting the poor of Jesus Christ. Let us then profit by so glorious an advantage; let us be faithful to this great and holy practice to which Heaven is promised as its eternal reward! In fine, *let us never neglect the visit of the poor at their abodes.*

General Regulations.

ARTICLE 1. All persons, of whatever country, who desire to participate in the prayers and good works of the Society of St. Vincent of Paul, will be cheerfully received as members of this charitable Association.

2. No work of charity within the power of a lay Catholic to render should be regarded as foreign to the Society, although its more especial object is to visit poor families at their own homes. Members may thus take every opportunity of affording consolation to the sick and imprisoned, of giving instruction to poor children, and

religious succour to those who need it at the hour of death.

3. When a certain number of persons become members of the Society in a town, they assemble together in order mutually to practice virtue. This association takes the name of *Conference*, under which name the Society began its existence.

4. When many Conferences are established in a town, they are distinguished by the names of the different localities in which they meet. They are united by a particular Council, which takes the name of the city in which it is established.

5. The different *Conferences* of the Society are united by a *General Council*.

CHAPTER I.

OF THE CONFERENCES.

6. The Conferences assemble on appointed days and hours.

7. The several Conferences of a town will correspond together in order to edify one another, and to recommend to each other the members of the Society, other young persons, or the poor families who often change their residence.

SECTION I.

ORGANIZATION OF THE CONFERENCES.

8. Each Conference has a President, one or more Vice-Presidents, a Secretary, and a Treasurer; these form the Board of the Conference.

Each Conference has also an Assistant-Secretary, an Assistant-Treasurer, a Keeper of the Records, a Keeper of the Register, a Librarian, a Patron of Schools, Trustees and Overseers of Sales, a Keeper of the Wardrobe, a Physician, Keepers of Provisions or Stores, Collectors and Porters, and any other officers who may be required.

9. The President is elected by the Conference. The other officers are named by the President, with the advice of the Board. However, as is said hereafter, (Ch. II., sec. 45) in cities where a Council of direction, or Particular Council exists, the Presidents and Vice-Presidents of the several Conferences are named by the President of the Council, and the admission of members to said Conferences is sanctioned by the said Council.

10. The President directs the Conference, receives and presents the propositions, calls the meetings if necessary, and superintends the execution of the rules and decisions of the Society.

In his absence, his place is taken by one of the Vice-Presidents.

11. The Secretary keeps the minutes of the meetings, and a register of the names, professions and abodes of the members, the dates of their reception, and the names of the persons by whom they have been presented. He also keeps a list indicating the names of the families who receive aid, their abodes, the names of the members who visit them, and the quantity and nature of assistance given to each of them.

D

He takes notes of the changes which occur in the families, and in those who visit them.

12. The Treasurer has the keeping of the money; at each meeting he takes an account of the receipts and disbursements.

13. The Keeper of the Records has the care of the different papers belonging to the Conference.

14. The Keeper of the Register inscribes the names of the poor who have no employment, in a register indicating the age, trade and abode of such persons. He also keeps note of the persons with whom they are placed by the Conference.

15. The Librarian collects instructive books, which he lends to the poor under the directions of the Conference, keeping a correct account of the same.

16. The Patron of Schools receives from the Secretary the names of the children patronized, visits their schools weekly, reports on their conduct to the Conference, and distributes the rewards granted to them.

17. The Trustees or Overseers of sales, take care of the different donations made to the Conference, for the benefit of which the articles are sold by auction or disposed of otherwise.

18. The Keeper of the wardrobe collects clothing for the use of the poor, and keeps a list of the articles, and to whom delivered.

19. The keepers of provisions or stores distribute the different articles they are intrusted with. They transmit to the Treasurer the tickets they receive, which they must not keep more than eight days.

20. The Collectors keep a list of the subscribers, receive their offerings at the periods fixed, and transmit them to the Treasurer.

21. The Porters have orders not to admit to the Conference any person who is not a member of the Society, unless introduced by a member

SECTION II.

ORDER OF MEETINGS.

22. At the opening of each meeting the President recites the prayer: "*Come Holy Ghost,*" followed by the orison and an invocation to St. Vincent of Paul. After which a lecture is made from some pious book; each member being invited to read in his turn.

23. The Secretary reads the minutes of the preceding meeting. Each member can make observations on these minutes.

24. The Treasurer publishes the amount of the funds, in order that demands for aid may be proportioned to the same.

25. If new members are to be received, the President proclaims the admission of candidates presented and announced at the three preceding meetings; it is the Secretary's duty to apprise them of their admission.

26. When a member wishes to introduce a candidate to the Conference, he must furnish the President with the name, calling and residence of the candidate, some days previous to the meeting, at which he may be proposed, in order that the President, *who is specially charged with the direction and the honour of the*

Conference, may enquire into the qualifications of the candidate, and present him for admission, if he be found to possess those Christian virtues that should guide the conduct of a member of the Society of St. Vincent of Paul. A person desirous of becoming a member of the Society, must be presented by two members. No candidate can be admitted into the Society without being published at four meetings of the Conferrence into which he desires admittance, and his reception as a member shall take place only after the fourth calling. Each member will take care to introduce into the Society those persons only who are capable of edifying it, and who are disposed to love their colleagues and the poor, as their brothers.

27. Members, who have any observations to make on the candidate, transmit them to the President in writing, or verbally, before the time shall have elapsed that precedes the meeting at which the candidate is to be admitted. If no observations be made, the candidate is received at the fifth meeting following that of his nomination.

28. If the person who is presented as a candidate belong to any secret, or other society condemned by the Church, he cannot be received as a member of the Conference. And if a member, after being received, join any society condemned by the Church, the Secretary shall write him an official letter, admonishing him to send in his resignation; and if he do not resign within a certain time, the Secretary shall give information thereof to the Conference.

29. A person not having means to contribute to the common funds, cannot be admitted as a member.

30. A member of the Society cannot, under any pretext or circumstance whatever, receive aid from its funds.

31. The President requests the members to give information regarding the families they were charged to visit, and reads the reports on the families proposed at the preceding meeting; before the vote of the Conference is taken, each member may make such observations on these reports as he thinks useful.

32. When the reports have been read, the President publishes the other families who demand help; and selects two of the oldest members to visit and examine each family proposed.

33. Tickets, donating the help granted to each family adopted, are then given, and they can be changed according to the wants of the poor. The Secretary calls the visitors, and points out the assistance which is granted to each family.

Assistance should invariably be given to the poor during the interval between each meeting. The time, the number, and the manner of these visits, are left to the prudence of the visitors, as are also the means to be adopted in order to introduce into families the love of religion and the practice of its duties.

Visitors who request rules of conduct, or advice in difficult circumstances, ought to be heard with attention and kindness; the President, or any other member, answers according as his experience and his charity may dictate.

34. If assistance in money, in clothes, or in books be requested, the motives of such requests ought to be developed, and the Conference votes accordingly.

When it is impossible to avoid a grant in money, by giving its equivalent in another form, the member, who has received this money, should watch as closely as possible, over the use which is made of it.

35. After determining the nature of the assistance about to be given, the attention of the Conference is occupied with the appointments to be made, the steps to be taken for the benefit of the poor, and such other interesting matters.

No new family is received without having been visited by two members named by the President; if the family is adopted, it is confided to the care of two other visitors ; a member who recommends a family cannot be named to visit it ; a ticket for one small loaf is given to the family thus visited.

36. Members, who are about to leave for a time or forever the Conference they belong to, inform the President, who confides to others the business with which they are charged.

37. The Conference then considers such means as may tend to its support, its growth, and the proper distribution of its funds.

38. If a poor person die, his death is announced at the next meeting, and the President invites the Conference to assist at a Mass which is said for the repose of his soul, on the first convenient

day; and at the end of the meeting the *De Profundis* is recited,

39. Before the closing prayers, the Treasurer, or whoever is charged with taking up the collection, (to which each member contributes according to his means, but *always secretly*), goes through the meeting for the purpose of doing so. Those who cannot sacrifice their time in serving the poor, endeavour to make amends by a greater pecuniary contribution. This collection is intended to meet the wants of the families visited; but members should not neglect any other proper means which may be available for increasing their funds.

40. The meeting closes by the Prayers " *For Benefactors,*" " *Most Gracious Jesus,*" and " *We fly to Thy Patronage,*" etc.

CHAPTER II.

OF PARTICULAR COUNCILS.

41. The Particular Council of a city is composed of a President, one or more Vice-Presidents; a Secretary, one or more Assistant-Secretaries; a Treasurer, one or more Assistant-Treasurers; all the Presidents and Vice-Presidents of the different Conferences of the city, and the Presidents and Vice-Presidents of such special objects of Charity as may interest them all.

42. The Particular Council occupies itself with those important measures of ways and means which interest all the Conferences of the city.

43. The Council decides in what manner the common fund is to be employed.

This fund is supported by charitable gifts from without, by collections made at the general meetings in the city, and by the offerings which at each Council Meeting, the Presidents bring in the name of their respective Conferences. It is destined to meet the general wants and to assist the poorer Conferences.

44. The President, Vice-Presidents, Secretary, and Treasurer, form an ordinary Council, to which belongs the direction of the usual business.

45. The President is named by the Council, with the advice of the Conferences. The first time, he is named by the united Conferences. The President nominates the Presidents and the Vice-Presidents of Conferences and of Special Works, as well as the Vice-President, the Secretary and Treasurer of the Particular Council, advising with his Council upon all these nominations.

46. The President of the Particular Council directs its proceedings, receives and presents the propositions, and calls the meetings if necessary. He presides over the general assemblies of the locality.

47. The Secretary keeps the minutes of the sittings of the Council, and a register of the names, professions and places of abode of all the members of the different Conferences of the city, with the date of their reception, and the names of those who presented them.

48. The Treasurer takes charge of the funds of the Council.

49. The Presidents and Vice-Presidents of Conferences represent their Conferences in the Particular Council. The Presidents of special works of Charity attend there to defend the interests of those works. The one and the other make reports, when invited to do so by the President of the Council.

CHAPTER III.

THE GENERAL COUNCIL.

50. The General Council is composed of a President, a Vice-President, a Secretary, and a Treasurer, with many Councillors.

51. The General Council is the link which binds together all the Conferences; it maintains the unity of the Society, superintends all that may tend to promote its prosperity, and puts into operation the decisions at which it arrives for that purpose.

52. It decides on the use to be made of the general fund, which is supported by extraordinary presents made to the Society, by collections at general meetings of the Society, and by the offerings which each Conference or each Council sends to defray the general expenses of the Society.

53. The members of the general Council are named by the President, with the advice of the Council.

54 When there is occasion to name a General President of the Society, the General Council is convoked by the Vice-President. This meeting, which is preparatory, is devoted to taking into consideration the merits of the persons who

might be charged with this important office. The former President is requested to point out some person whom he may think worthy of election.

After maturely reflecting on the choice of one or more persons, the meeting adjourns for two months. In the interval, advice is given of this preliminary meeting to the Presidents of Particular Councils, who consult their colleagues ; and to those of Conferences, who consult their Officers, or even the Conferences they direct ; they all transmit their opinions to the General Council ; on these opinions the election is made, of which correct minutes are taken.

While the election lasts, all the members of the Society, either in private or at their meetings, address a prayer to God, viz: the *"Veni Creator,"* in order that His Holy Spirit may enlighten them in the choice they are about to make.

55. The General President, if necessary, calls extraordinary meetings ; he presides over those meetings, and also over the General Council.

56. The General Secretary keeps an account of the names, professions, and places of residence of the members, together with the dates of their admission ; he also keeps an account of the Boards of Councils or Conferences, and of the places, days and hours of their meetings.

He prepares the minutes of the sittings of the General Council and of the General Meetings.

He edits the annual report on the state of the Society's proceedings.

He has charge of the general correspondence with the Provincial and Particular Presidents or Secretaries of the Councils or Conferences.

He keeps the Records of the Society.

57. The General Treasurer keeps the funds. He puts in order the receipts and expenses and submits his accounts to the General Council.

58. A member of the General Council is charged by the General President with the Presidency of the Council, if he cannot preside over it himself; another member is also named by him, on the proposition of the General Secretary, to fill the duties of Vice-Secretary.

CHAPTER IV.

GENERAL MEETINGS.

59. The General Meetings are held each year, on the 8th of December, (the feast of the Immaculate Conception of the Blessed Virgin;) the first Sunday in Lent; the second Sunday after Easter, (Anniversary of the Translation of the Relics of St. Vincent of Paul); and on the 19th of July, the feast of this Holy Patron.

The President can, besides, convoke extraordinary General Meetings.

60. The General Meetings commence, like those of Conferences, by the usual prayers and a pious lecture.

61. After having read the minutes of the last General Meeting, the Secretary calls over the names of members received since, which names have been transmitted to him by the Presidents of the Conferences.

62. The President then gives a summary statement of the transactions of the Society,

himself addresses the meeting, or invites one of the members to do so.

63. One of the Vice-Secretaries then reads a report on the state of the Conferences.

A summary of the report, pointing out the movements of members, or poor families, and the amount of the receipts and expenses, is placed in the hands of the Secretary.

64. The President then makes known the decisions which the Council of Direction has adopted in matters connected with the welfare of the Society, and consults, if necessary, the meeting itself.

The Society deems itself happy when persons recommendable by their character, their virtue, or their learning, have the kindness, on the invitation of the President, to assist at the General Meeting, and terminate it by some edifying remarks.

65. After the usual collection and prayers, the meeting separates.

CHAPTER V.

OF THE DIFFERENT MEMBERS OF THE SOCIETY.

66. Besides the ordinary members of the Conferences, who take an active part in all its proceedings, the Society has corresponding members, honorary members, and subscribers.

67. When a member of the Society changes his residence, if there is no Conference in the city, or place to which he goes, he does not, on that account cease to be a member, but takes the

title of corresponding member ; he enters into communication with the Conference, or Conferences of the city near which he resides, and corresponds with the Secretary of the Council, or Conference of that city. When there is no Conference in the Diocese, he corresponds with the General Secretary. He receives each year a report on the objects of Charity of the Society, and remains in community with it, not only of prayers, but also of good works ; accomplishing around him works of charity, and making himself useful to the Society, whenever an opportunity presents.

68. Honorary members may assist at the Conferences, but they have no vote. They ought to send each year a special offering to the Treasurer of the Council, or the Conference of their city.

The reception of honorary members is made in the same manner as that of ordinary members ; in towns where many Conferences are established, it is made by the Particular Council.

69. Each Conference can have subscribers, likewise.

Subscribers are not members of the Society, but in their quality of benefactors, they have a claim on its prayers.

CHAPTER VI.

OF THE FEASTS OF THE SOCIETY.

70. The Society celebrates the Feast of the

Immaculate Conception of the Blessed Virgin, 8th December : of St. Vincent of Paul, its Patron, 19th July ; and of the anniversary of the Translation of the Relics of St. Vincent of Paul, 2nd Sunday after Easter. On these days the Conferences attend in a body at Mass, and pray for the prosperity of the Catholic Faith, and for the increase of Charity among men, in order to bring upon their works the Divine benediction. If a member cannot attend, he, at least, unites in intention with his brethren and prays for them as they pray for him.

71. The day after the General Assembly of Lent, all the members of the Society assist in a body at a *Requiem* Mass, which is celebrated for the repose of the souls of deceased members and benefactors of the Society.

Observations.

None of the obligations imposed by these Rules are binding in conscience ; but the Society confides their accomplishment to the zeal of its members, and to their love of God and of their neighbour. Moreover, it will be remarked that mention is made only of young men ; but persons advanced in age have joined the Conferences. Besides, youths cannot remain separate from other members who have advanced in years ; there is, therefore, a mixture in the Society which is useful for the interest of the poor and the stability of the Conferences. However, in certain districts of Paris, and in provincial towns which possess the opportunity, the Conferences remain entirely composed of young men. Finally, time has already introduced modifications to the Rules, according to the locality and development of the work, but the foundation remains ; each Conference adheres to it as closely as possible ; and the spirit which presided over the foundation of the Society and dedicated these preliminary remarks, is in no manner departed from.

By following these rules, which at first were but mere customs, the Christian youth, who form a part of the Society, have endeavoured to obtain the following double object, viz :

To learn to know and love one another.

To learn to know, love, and assist the poor of Jesus Christ.

The establishment of several Conferences has not been an obstacle to the accomplishment of this two-fold object ; Christian intimacy has even become greater between members of the same section, than would be possible between all the members of the Society united in one Conference. One is never so much alone as in a crowd, and large meetings in this respect resemble a crowd, which bustles and passes on, in which we take no interest and which takes no interest in us. Besides, a correspondence is carried on, from time to time, with distant Conferences. Those of the same city occasionally meet together, and these meetings and letters, bind us more closely in the bonds of fraternal charity. Neither distance nor any other obstacle can impede that friendship which is founded on a community of prayers and charitable works.

Let us then take courage ; united or separated, far or near, let us love one another, let us love and assist the poor. Let us love this little Society which has made us known to one another, and which has opened to us the prospect of a more charitable and Christian life. Let us love our customs and our rules ; if we observe them faithfully, we may rest assured that they will protect us, and protect our work. " Much evil is committed," said a venerable priest to another charitable society, " let us endeavour to do a little good." Oh ! how we shall one day rejoice at not having allowed our youthful years to glide uselessly along ! Youth is a field which requires cultivation. Let us not then hurry over it, without indulging in wholesome thoughts of the future ; let us cast an eye on every side around us ; let us gather with care the ears of corn that lie scattered at our feet ; *let us do some good;* it will be the sheaf of our provision through life ; it will yield us a plentiful harvest before the Lord.

INSTRUCTIONS TO BE FOLLOWED

IN FORMING

Conferences of St. Vincent of Paul.

PEOPLE, who have never borne an active part in the meetings of the Society of St. Vincent of Paul, frequently form a false idea concerning the difficulties of founding a Conference. To clear away all errors on such a point, it will be well to explain, in a few words, in what our Society principally consists, and to state by what practical means Conferences have been hitherto founded. We shall, perhaps, furnish many with matter for reflecting, and seriously examining whether it be in their power to endow the town they inhabit with such a useful institution.

As has been often said, the Conferences of St. Vincent of Paul are not, necessarily, designed to relieve *a vast number of poor*. Such a result would, doubtless, be a source of happiness to them, but it is neither an obligation, nor a necessary condition for existence. Their chief object is, the sanctification of the members by the personal performance of acts of charity, which may be accomplished as easily by the humblest Conference, as by the most numerous and wealthy one. Whence spring several consequences, which lead us immediately to our subject.

The first is, that those, who wish to found a Conference, should not be deterred by the fewness of willing helpers they meet with. The Confererence, out of which all others sprang, viz : that of Paris, was founded by 8 members, that of London, by 13, that of Caën, by 3, that of Toronto, by 7 :—all of these are now in a flourishing state, and have given rise to many others. Nor is it necessary that people of high station should lend their influence to recommend a newly founded Conference to public attention. The humblest beginnings, as daily experience shows, often prove the best.

The second consequence is, that established *Societies* should not apprehend a dangerous rivalry from the formation of a Conference. The Society of St. Vincent of Paul has often pointed out the necessity of new Works, and furthered the foundation of many.* Up to the present day, *the Society has caused none to decline, nor diminished the prosperity of any*. The field of charity is so vast, that the gleaners who arrive latest will always find employment for all their time, and all their strength; to exercise their zeal, they can, at any time, adopt some ten or twenty families, without interfering with any public

---

* The Society of St. Vincent of Paul, which is exclusively composed of men, carefully avoids those Works which concern the other sex, and leaves them entirely to Female Societies. But in order that there may be no gap left in the organization of charity, it has often contributed, by its counsels and exhortations to found Sisterhoods, for the patronage of orphan or apprentice girls, etc., etc.

charitable institution, or with venerable Sisterhoods, parochial committees or other labourers in the work of love; and thus the zeal of the members may always be sufficiently stimulated.

Thirdly, it is by no means necessary to be able to rely on fixed resources. A Society that announces itself with pomp, and that declares its intention to relieve a whole class of poor, must necessarily find means for insuring certain and adequate revenues, in order to expect success. But when a Conference is small in number, as it may with impunity be, it may live, as it were, on its daily bread, following the advice of Tobias : *If you have much, give abundantly ; if you have little, take care even so to bestow willingly a little.* Tob. iv. 9.

Objections that oftentimes prevent the establishment of Conferences are thus done away with by a simple observation. If the chief object of the Society had been well known, many towns would have had their Conference of St. Vincent of Paul long since, and the Catholic youth and the poor would be now enjoying the benefits of the institution.

But let us enter upon the details of organization, and see if it be possible to make them thoroughly understood.

We have already said that a Conference, particularly at its outset, need not have many members; it is however essential that all the members composing it should be animated with a fitting spirit, for which it is not only requisite that each should be a sincere and practical Catholic, acting up to all the precepts of his Religion, but also that he should have studied the customs, traditions and habits of our Society. If then, any one wishing to undertake the establishment of a conference has no practical knowledge of the way of proceeding, his first care should be, to make himself thoroughly acquainted with the publications in which the Society has endeavoured to express its spirit, and describe its way of proceeding; particularly the General Regulations, whose preamble is almost entirely taken from the writings of Saint Vincent of Paul. After the Conference has been fairly established should doubts arise in its working, one may then read with profit, the Circulars of the General Presidents of the Society,—where practical solutions of the most usual difficuities are given,—and the General Reports, where the precepts of our Rule are illustrated and confirmed by examples.* Without studying these, it is to be feared that, however well disposed he may be, a person will fall into the very difficulties which the first brethren found it no easy thing to get out of; and it is also to be feared, that, under the name of Conferences of St. Vincent of Paul, societies would be formed resembling them but in name, and unable to meet the conditions attached to the Indulgences.

The preliminary study will not be a long task for a sincere Christian. As soon as it is accomplished, he must look around him for persons likely to assist him in founding a Conference; and when he thinks he has found them, he should

---

* Compendious extracts from these and other publications of the Society will be found in the " MANUAL."

submit the Rule to them, and ask them if they are willing to enter into the spirit of it, and to adopt its principles. But he must on no account apply to any but sincere Christians—Catholics who do not blush at performing all the duties commanded by the Church. Sad experience has proved the danger of not strictly adhering to this advice, and of admitting even charitably disposed people, however religious their feelings may be, if they hesitate at complying with *all* the precepts of the Church. A contrary line of conduct has always sown in Conferences the seed of dissension—perhaps, of dissolution.

A few other precautions are necessary for ensuring the prosperity of a Conference. Even the sincere performance of the external duties of Christianity does not suffice to make people fit to establish a Conference. With these duties they should unite enlightened and thorough piety, a spirit of conciliation, peace and humility, ardent love for the poor and for the Society and a perseverance undaunted by the difficulties inherent to all beginnings. They must bear in mind that they are destined to be the elders of the Conference, to whom the younger brethren will look for example and traditions; wherefore they should possess such qualities as will be edifying at all times, and in all places. Such members are fortunately more easily found than is generally supposed; so far are they from being confined to a certain class or station of life, that experience has fully proved that the closest intimacy, and most heartfelt affection, reign in those Conferences, where the ages, position and education of the members vary most. It can be affirmed, beyond contradiction, that in all the Conferences of Paris, as of many other cities and towns, the mixture of elements the most opposite, in a worldly sense, but united in the spirit of charity, has been attempted, practised, and continued, with pleasure and success.

It is frequently found that timid and circumspect people, are afraid to make engagements that bind them down or disturb the ordinary course of their lives. All such objections cannot be overruled, but one means should not be left untried, since it has often succeeded in such cases—*admit them to the Conference on trial.* If they have any zeal, the hindrances and difficulties they apprehend will soon vanish ; their desire to return to the meetings will triumph over difficulties, and their worldly occupations will square with the duties of charity ; thus, the Conference shall have acquired the co-operation of valuable members, who will contribute to its present and future welfare.

Thus in every rank of society, and in different political parties, are found desirable members, united in relieving the poor of our Blessed Lord, and advancing on the road to Christian perfection.

As a last step, before installing a Conference, the sanction of the Archbishop or Bishop of the Diocese in which it may be situated should be obtained.

Some Conferences, particularly those in Great Britain and Ireland, are wont to beg the ecclesiastical authority, to appoint a priest to be their spiritual director. Such a practice merits attention ; it preserves the lay character of the Society, strengthens the tie that binds it to the Church ; and ensures in all questions relating to the moral and religious state of the poor, the advice of a prudent and devoted guide.

It must be borne in mind that though we are laymen, we are also, and intend to remain, obedient Christians, and respectful sons of the Church.

In some places our brethren have been so fortunate as to induce their Bishop, or the Parish Priest, to accept the title of honorary president ; all these customs, though differing in form, tend to the same end ; they evince our unanimous desire to rally under our legitimate pastors,—the priests of the Church.

As soon as such sanction is obtained, the Conference should meet immediately, and set to work.

At this particular point, some Conferences have lost much precious time in discussing Rules and Regulations, under the idea that local considerations required some departure from certain customs enumerated in the General Regulations. Persons about to organize a Conference, cannot be too earnestly advised not to proceed thus, for, in the first place, it is evident, that Regulations that have stood so long a trial and have been approved by successive Popes, have many claims to confidence ; and, secondly, it can be safely affirmed from experience, that the right moment for laying down Rules is not at the outset of an undertaking ; at such a time arguments are based upon opinions only, and not on experience, and people are carried away by vague theories ;—" when," according to one of our brethren, who had followed such a path, " we think we have mountains before us, we shall, if we advance boldly, find that they sink under our feet." Pride also will but too often lead us to enter into preliminary discussions. Both sides are apt to get warm, and then obstinate, so that the first trial of a Conference of *Charity* is liable to be fraught with danger to that capital virtue. Lastly, it was not so that Saint Vincent of Paul, the Guide and Patron of our Society, acted. The order of virtuous priests that he founded, waited long for their written Regulations. It was only after years of experience, that he converted time-sanctioned customs into obligatory rules. Let us, then, follow our great patron's example, and be careful to imitate it when we help to found a Conference. Practice alone can show with certainty, what modification the General Regulations require. Alterations, justified by experience, are always the best.

Our new brethren should lose no time in appointing their officers ; concerning whose nomination rules are laid down in the General Regulations (page 32) ; to these rules they will do well to conform even in appointing provisional officers. It frequently happens that during the first few days members do not know one another well enough to be able to proceed to the final election of a President and other officers. On this point, their line of conduct must be determined by circumstances; for whilst in one case, the immediate and final appointment of a President, will secure the prosperity of a Conference, in another it may be prudent to wait for the arrival of new brethren, who can give more time and weight to the Society. Moreover, when the election is about to take place, we cannot too earnestly engage our confrères to follow the instructions given at page 63, where the qualities which make a good President are pointed out; gentleness of temper; a sincere and ardent affection for the Conference, its members, and its poor; an equal dislike for rash novelties, and for the spirit of routine; he should, if possible, be in independent circumstances, that all his energy may be devoted to the common work; and lastly, but above all, he should be endued with wisdom, prudence and an active mind.

After the installation of the officers, the day and place of meeting should be immediately fixed. A Conference that meets in a public building, be it a church, or a school-house, or a town-hall, is more likely to attract attention than one which meets in a private room. It is a great disadvantage to a Conference to be indebted for its place of meeting to the precarious good will of a person who is not a member; moreover, the necessity of going to the house of a person with whom one is not acquainted will frequently, particularly in country places, be made a pretext for not joining the Society, and the Conference may languish for want of a proper place of meeting. Our confrères should, then, hasten to find such a place; but it must be understood that the search should not last long enough to endanger the regularity of the meetings.

These preliminaries should be settled at the first meeting ; and in any event, it is highly important that the members should not separate, for the first time, without having put their hand to the plough by adopting some families, fixing upon the tradesmen who are to supply the provisions, &c., to be given to the poor, and by agreeing, at least temporarily, on the extent and nature of the relief to be given. Thus, entering immediately into practical existence, the members will be bound to the Conference; not one of them, if he has any charity in his heart, and, if in the interval he has visited a sick, or an infirm fellow creature, will fail to be present at the next meeting. Differences of opinion about charity, about the manner of relieving, and about theories, will give way before questions of practice, and a constantly increasing energy will spring up.

It will have been remarked that in earnestly recommending our confrères to hasten to adopt some work of charity, we mentioned the visitation of the poor at their homes ; and we did so designedly, for it is a work that, more than any other, becomes our Society. There are many special works of the Society, such as the Patronage of apprentices, Savings Banks for the poor, Orphan Asylums and the like which though very desirable, cannot be immediately undertaken on account of the time, the study, the capital they require ; but visiting the poor may, on the contrary, be set about without delay ; all that is necessary is to ask the Parish Priest, the Sisters of Charity, or benevolent people, for the names of a few poor families, who may be visited immediately, their wants inquired into, and relief given. It is then expedient that this precious work should be organized without loss of time; it is a work that may be done by all; it requires neither much time, nor much learning, nor much personal exertion, and may justly be called the daily bread of charity.

Another important point to be settled without delay is the regular weekly recurrence of the meetings. If Conferences meet but at long intervals, the interests of the poor will assuredly suffer, as it will be much more difficult to communicate to the members that uniformity of feeling and views with which alone a Conference can prosper; for we must bear in mind, that no work can prosper that does not frequently engage us. Another still more capital point is to open and close the sittings with the usual prayers, and to establish the custom of making a collection with inviolable secrecy. Indeed, without offering up our prayers, we should run the risk of forgetting that we meet in the name of Jesus Christ, and that we can have no merit that does not spring from Him; without *absolute secrecy* in making the collection, or with the principle of fixed contributions for members, we should deprive ourselves of one of the most precious merits of alms-giving, that of joining humility to sacrifice.

When all these preparatory measures are completed, the Conference is founded, and must rely on the grace of God, on the zeal of its members, and on time, for future extension. It may then notify its existence to the General Council, and solicit aggregation, which will assure to it the spiritual favours granted so liberally to the Society by venerable Popes. Until the formation of a Superior Council for Ontario at Toronto, the Superior Council of Quebec will be the medium of communication between all Councils and Conferences of this Province and the Council General at Paris. The petition should be made without any set formality, in the simple and homely way that characterizes our dealings and correspondence; it will suffice to make known to the Council the following points, entering, of course, into all details likely to interest or edify :—

1. The date of the foundation of the Conference;
2. The name of the Patron Saint of the Conference;
3. The list of the officers, with their professions or occupations, and their addresses;
4. The names of the other members of the Conference;
5. The days, time and place of meeting;
6. The works chosen;
7. The adoption of the General Regulations.

We will suppose the Conference duly incorporated into our family of charity; it must now hasten to reap the advantages of such a communion of prayer, works and thoughts. The General Reports, the Circulars of the General

Assemblies, the Reports of brother Conferences, and the frequent periodical perusal of our *Bulletin* will quickly unite the new Conference to its numerous brethren ; but nothing will be found so efficacious as frequent correspondence with the General and Provincial Councils, and communication by word or letter with neighbouring Conferences. Thus by a mutual communication of thoughts and deeds, and by heartfelt piety, the first fervour of zeal is kept up, whilst progress is being made in experience and wisdom.

Such are the means that have been employed for founding Conferences. This simple notice will, we hope, justify the observation we set out with, and show how easy it is to extend and multiply the branches of our dear Society. May they continue to be multiplied to the edification of Catholic men and youths and to the relief of the poor ! May these hints, by drawing the attention of all our confreres to old established rules, contribute to maintain that unity which is the offspring of fraternal charity and verify the motto : *Deus est qui inhabitare facit unanimes in domo* Ps. lxvii, 7.

INSTRUCTIONS

ON THE

Duties of Presidents and Vice-Presidents

OF

COUNCILS AND CONFERENCES.

REASONS FOR THIS WORK.

THE President is the soul of the Council or Conference over which he is placed, and as his knowledge of the duties of his office is little or great, so also is the influence which he exercises over his charge. For this reason it has been judged useful to present to Presidents and Vice-Presidents, the nearly complete view of the obligations attached to their respective offices, contained in the following instructions, taken chiefly from the fundamental rules, usages, and traditions of our Society. Though principally intended for Presidents and Vice-Presidents, they will be found equally useful to all other members, affording them opportunities of reviving in their hearts the primitive spirit of our institution, of which we are more apt to lose sight, as each year removes us further from its foundation.

May the ever Immaculate Virgin and our Holy Patron, St. Vincent, procure for these pages the graces and blessings which will enable them to produce salutary effects.

CONDITIONS IN THE CHOICE OF A PRESIDENT.

Nothing is of more importance to the well-being of a work than the choice of a President. St. Vincent of Paul used to say, that if, in an enterprise, he was obliged to choose between fifty stags commanded by a lion, or fifty lions commanded by a stag, he would depend more for success on the former phalanx than on the latter; the leader being, in his mind, a consideration of the utmost importance. It will, therefore, be necessary for us to consider first, the *Signs by which we may recognize a person likely to make a good President.*—The member who considers the position of President as a charge rather than an honour, who is neither eager in seeking for it, nor too ready to accept it, has already given some evidence that he is worthy of being appointed. With these dispositions he should unite a happy mixture of mildness and firmness, a sincere and ardent affection for the Society, for its members and for the poor; a disinclination equally for ill-advised novelties and for the mere spirit of routine; if possible, a sufficiently independent position to permit of his devoting his time, his strength, and his mind to the work; activity, constancy, prudence, and wisdom; and to crown, or rather to enliven all, a true piety, tolerant and universal, which will diffuse itself through his actions, and draw down blessings and graces from above.

The consideration attached to a person on account of age, position, influence, or fortune, should not determine the choice of a President; at most, such qualities may, in certain cases, form motives for a preference between two candidates, and then only where the greater good of the Society is to be consulted; but that which we must seek for, above all, is a Christian spirit, the spirit of charity, the spirit of St. Vincent of Paul.

DUTIES OF THE PRESIDENT IN ENTERING ON HIS FUNCTIONS.

Reading of the Rules, the Manual, Circulars and the Bulletin.—A thorough acquaintance with the spirit, rules, objects and even history of a work, is indispensably necessary to its proper conduct. Every President, therefore, who is about to enter on his functions, will do well to acquaint himself with his work by attentively studying the Rules, the Manual, the Circulars, and the *Bulletin*, and the more frequently he resumes this reading, especially that of the *Bulletin*—the recognized organ of the Council General—the better will he identify himself with the spirit which imparts life and vigour to our operations, familiarize himself with their practical details, and be enabled to carry them out.

Study of the condition of the Works of Conferences.—The President, if of a Conference, ought to ascertain everything relating to its state, or, if of a Council, everything relating to the Conferences and general works of the circumscription ; and for this purpose he ought to have recourse to personal inquiries and personal information, as well as to any correspondence originating either with himself or his predecessors. After such inquiries he will be able, more clearly, to steer his course and shape his conduct.

DUTIES OF THE PRESIDENT AT THE MEETINGS OF HIS CONFERENCE.

Assiduity, punctuality.—Assiduity and punctuality are qualities very necessary in a President ; his negligence on these points would retard the progress of the work, and even endanger its existence, by paralysing the energies and discouraging the zeal of the members, over whom he will soon lose all active influence and authority.

Order of the Meetings.—He should take care that the business of each meeting is properly arranged, and should come with a prepared programme, which, while following the general order laid down by the Rules, should be so varied in the details, as to avoid both confusion and monotony. The time of the meetings will thus be usefully filled up, and they will not be found tedious ; care should be taken to occupy only a reasonable time, for long and wearisome meetings are seldom profitable ; while on the other hand, cordial, gay and friendly meetings are useful both to the members and to the poor ; cheerfulness is exceedingly advantageous; it excites attention, prevents drowsiness, favours cordiality, and discourages dissension.

Duty of the President in originating works.—The President should equally avoid originating too much himself, or leaving too much to others. He should neither pull the reins too tight, nor leave them too loose. He should regulate or moderate the liberty of each member, but not unduly restrain, still less entirely ignore it. He should expedite simple details, such as the allocation of assistance to poor families, and not allow precious time to be consumed in fruitless conversation, as is too often the case; he should prevent useless discussion, even on grave subjects, and remind the members that they have met, not for debate, but for mutual edification, and to work together for the glory of God and the benefit of the poor. In serious and useful discussions, however, from which some profitable suggestions or decisions may result, he will allow the most free expression of opinion so long as it does not wander into useless digression, or degenerate into personality; he will afford the members time to state their views, proceeding in order, and inviting those who are so desirous, to speak in turn. These having spoken, he will close the discussion, review the principal points, give his own opinion, and put the matter to the vote. Should his opinion be contradicted or opposed, he will not show resentment or bitterness, but accept with cheerfulness the decision of the majority. In order to obtain guidance in difficult questions, he should take beforehand the opinion of the Board of his Conference, and if he think fit, of particular members.

Essential portions of the business of a President at a Meeting.—There are some other details which greatly affect the good order of the meeting. The President should insist on strict silence being observed during the time of pious reading at the commencement of the meeting; and the chapter chosen by him for reading should be short, interesting and practical. He should remind members who arrive after the opening prayer has been said, that they should recite it apart and on their knees, one of the objects of our meetings being public prayer. He should take care that all the acts which, in a manner form the working of a Conference— such as communications by correspondence or otherwise, reports of visitors, the distribution of relief, the bag collection, &c.,—should come on, each in its turn, and as much as possible in the accustomed order, so that this regularity may become habitual, and confusion and loss of time be avoided.

Communications to the Conference.—As regards the communications which ought to be made to the Conference, the President should not omit to read the general recommendations of the *Bulletin*, which nearly always convey important information on the Rules and Works of the Society; it is even very desirable that each number of the *Bulletin* should be read in the interval between one month's publication and the next; this would prevent omissions and negligence, which often retard the progress of a Conference.

DUTIES OF PRESIDENTS IN REGARD TO THE CONFERENCE OR THE COUNCIL.

Some general points are common to Presidents of Conferences and of Councils.

Giving effect to decisions.—When a decision has been given, the duty of the President is to carry, or cause it to be carried, into effect, and that immediately, as delay often compromises success. How many opportunities of doing good, or of establishing a Conference, have been lost from not having been seized on at the favourable moment.

Introduction of New Works.—Before introducing new works into a Conference or Council, the President, having first implored the light of the Holy Ghost, should carefully examine which will be the best to undertake; for this end he must study the dispositions of the members, the wants of the locality, the resources which will be necessary for carrying on, as well as those which can be realized for the proposed work, and above all, the good that may be effected by it. In making this examination he should equally guard against too much confidence or too much timidity; excessive confidence leads to hazardous or short-lived enterprises, while on the other hand, excessive prudence is often the result of disguised apathy and inconstancy.

Exciting a spirit of piety.—The President should particularly strive to excite a spirit of piety around him, first by his example, next by appropriate advice occasionally given, but always in a general manner ; thus he might remind the members of the high dignity of the poor, and of the excellence of our mission among them ; he might frequently mention the Indulgences attached to the works of the Society ; he should watch over the punctual celebration of the feasts, and use his utmost endeavours to introduce the custom of spiritual retreats, and other works of zeal. He must, however, recollect that such piety is recommended, not commanded, and whilst taking every means to increase it amongst the members, he should maintain a wise discretion in his words and actions.

Choice of Members of the Board of the Conference.—The choice of the Vice-Presidents, Secretary and Treasurer (who with himself form the Board of the Conference), and all the other officers belongs to the President, except that where a Particular Council is established, the nomination of Vice-Presidents is reserved to it. In general, persons who have the most time and money at their disposal, are too readily selected as members of the Board,—without ascertaining if they combine the efficiency and zeal, which would make them truly useful. As they are called to take part in the government of the Conference, it is of the utmost importance to know beforehand what information they possess, and what services they will be able to render.

Importance of the Meetings of the Board of the Conference.-- It is in these meetings that little details of business are arranged, important questions prepared and discussed, and delicate matters, which could not well be entered into at the Conference, examined ; there the President's mind is enlightened and fortified, and his authority is confirmed ; in a word, from these meetings proceed the happiest results. Hence it is of the utmost importance to choose with care the members of the Board and to hold its meetings regularly and frequently.

Correspondence.—Correspondence is also a duty common to all Presidents ; it is one of the most precious safeguards of the unity of our Society and revives and keeps alive its spirit. If a Conference cease to correspond with the Council of its circumscription, we may at once consider its existence in peril ; if a Council suspend its correspondence, it is a sure sign that the life of that Council is gradually becoming extinct. The President of a Conference should therefore attend regularly the meetings of the Particular Council where one is established ; if there be no Particular Council, he should frequently correspond with the Provincial (or in its absence the General) Council, and make known to it through periodical reports all the circumstances connected with his works. The President of a Council, being the ordinary medium of communication, should keep up an intimate connection on the one hand with the Conferences of his circumscription, and on the other with the Provincial or General Council. The periodical interchange of statistical reports serves to main-maintain this mutual intimacy, and the more active and regular it is, the more prosperous and multiplied are the works.

Sharing with the members the Correspondence—A President, sometimes, finds the correspondence too laborious, and requires some one to share the labour with him. He should then choose assistants from the members of his Board, especially the Vice-Presidents and the Secretaries; it is a good way of teaching them the business, and rendering them able to direct and preside over the work in his absence. But in order to maintain unity of direction, especially in important affairs, the President should be careful always to originate the resolutions to be passed and the decisions to be made.

PARTICULAR DUTIES OF THE PRESIDENT OF CONFERENCES.

We come now to the duties which principally devolve on Presidents of Conferences:

Admission of members.—In the admission of members, Presidents are sometimes too easy and careless; at other times, but more rarely, too strict and exclusive. They should steer a medium course between these two excesses. The President should take care that no proposal of a member be made to the Conference but through him; to him the candidates, or the members who present them, should first address themselves; and no one but the President should propose the candidates at the Conference meeting ; the Rule is express on this point, and cannot be too strictly observed.

Points to be examined in choosing a member.—With respect to each candidate, the President should principally inquire: 1st, if he be likely to honour his faith by the practice of a Christian life ; 2nd, if he be in a situation to relieve the poor, however slightly. This latter condition should be insisted on almost as strictly as the former, otherwise admission to the Conference would be sought by persons anxious to receive relief rather than to give it.

Besides these two principal points, the President should ascertain if the social position and known antecedents of the candidate, or certain faults in his character or temper, will not cause his presence at the Conference to produce trouble, difficulty, or want of union.

Recruiting the Conferences.—The President should, as much as possible, seek for new members amongst young people, as well on account of the primitive objects and duration and development of our works, as for the moral and religious benefits young men receive in the Society.

No difficulty exists in doing this ; for, the circumscription of a Conference being necessarily small, persons know each other well, and when a young man is of proper age, the President should go to him, communicate with his family, show them the nature of the Society and the religious advantages that a young man is sure to obtain. He will thus have no trouble in gaining a new member to the Conference, and do good to all parties.

Reason of the difficulty found in recruiting Conferences.—It may be here remarked incidentally, that if, in general, difficulty is found in recruiting Conferences, it is because the Society is not sufficiently well known to Christian people; how many are there who, if they were only aware of the objects of the Society, the results attained by it, and the Indulgences attached to a participation in its works, as active, honorary, or aspirant members, or even simply as benefactors, would hasten to join it in one capacity or another? This point deserves the attention of Presidents. Frequently, also, young men do not receive that cordial welcome of which they are so sensible, and which is so necessary to attract them to our Society. Under pretence of their youth, they are kept at a distance; no advance is made towards them, and they are not given any employment in the Conference. This is a great error, and if many Conferences have but few young members, the fact may be attributed to this icy reserve, so contrary to the spirit of the Society. The President should also be careful to provide every new member with a copy of the Rules; for people unacquainted with them can take no permanent interest in the operations of our association. A new member should also be employed without delay in visiting the poor, and one of his more experienced confreres should be named as his companion.

A President should make himself acquainted with the circumstances of the poor.—Next to a personal knowledge of the members, a knowledge of the poor requires a President's particular care; it is essential, both in a moral and material point of view, that he should make himself acquainted with them as much as possible; otherwise, there will not be a proper distribution of families amongst the members, and but little efficacy in the assistance given. In this distribution of families the age, position and character of the visiting members must be considered ; by this care the visitor and the poor family will benefit each other. The President will acquire this knowledge of the poor families, either by visiting them periodically at least once a year—or by visiting for a certain time, those who have been lately placed on the list.

Duties of Presidents with regard to Special Works.—When a Conference, placed outside the immediate control of a Council, adopts special works, the President should have his eye and his hand over these works, without, however, constituting himself the sole director, lest in the event of his resignation of office, the members should become embarrassed and less zealous; he will watch over their proper direction, and will take care that they do not deviate from the rules, customs, or spirit of the Society; for this reason, he will always keep in view the proceedings, either by joining in the works himself, or by requiring an account occasionally, from those who direct them.

Special Works suited to Rural Conferences.—In rural Conferences, where, sometimes, there are but few poor families to be visited, the President should direct the energy of the members to works likely to develope and excite their zeal

—attending the sick, instructing children, the patronage of schools, teaching catechism, placing and watching over children in pious families, distributing good books, pious reading during the winter evenings, sowing and cultivating land belonging to poor or sick families—these are some of the works with which a rural Conference, however small, may always be occupied. To this end the President should communicate with the Parish Priest, in order to select those works which will best suit the wants of the parish, and the abilities of the members.

Conduct of the President in difficulties.—When beset by difficulties, of a nature likely to depress or injure the progress of the Conference, the President should first prepare himself by recollection and prayer, in order to bring to his aid all the circumspection, prudence and judgment, necessary to carry him through. If a difficulty, whatever be its origin, arise in the Conference, he should beware of allowing it to be known outside, lest it cause scandal. Having taken the opinion of the Board, and, if necessary, of those members whose experience and virtue bear most weight in the Conference; having, moreover, if the case be serious, referred it to the Council of the circumscription, or to the Council-General, he will determine what should be done, and will endeavour, both in taking and carrying out the proper measures, to act in the most conciliatory manner, and with discretion and charity.

Should difficulties arise externally, for example, from attacks in the public papers, false reports, or even hostile denunciations, the President, in order to maintain peace and calmness in the Conference, and to prevent rash and hasty resolutions, will avoid speaking of the matter at the meetings ; he will turn the thoughts of the members from it, endeavouring by personal and prudent efforts, and verbal explanations to justify the work, show it in its true colours, and so appease or avert the storm ; he will surely succeed much better in this manner than by angry altercation. If, however, he should fail in thus setting matters right, he ought to take the advice of the Council of the circumscription, and, if necessary, of the Council-General ; he should also appeal to well-informed prudent persons, and to the clergy, and he could then, with more confidence and safety, come to a proper conclusion.

SPECIAL DUTIES OF PRESIDENTS OF COUNCILS.

The advice of the Council of the circumscription, or of the General Council, should be received with respect by a Conference ; but this does not prevent them from making upon it any observations which they may think proper. On the other hand, this advice should be given, not in a tone of authority, but as a cordial warning. The President who speaks or writes in the name of a Council should, therefore, carefully avoid every expression which would seem to conv y an injunction or an order—and confine himself to words of mildness and persuasion, mingled when necessary, with those of firmness.

A President should make himself well acquainted with the Conferences and the Works of the Circumscription.—As the President of a Conference should make himself well acquainted with the members and the poor families, in like manner the President of a Council should have a general knowledge of the Conferences and the Works of his circumscription. If it be not extensive, in the case, for instance, of a particular Council, this knowledge will be easily acquired by regularly and frequently visiting the Conferences; if, on the contrary, it be a Superior or Central Council, and if the circumscription be too large to allow of the President visiting the Conferences regularly, he should send to those which are the farthest from him, either some member of the Council or the President of the Particular Council, or even the President of one of the nearest Conferences. And that these visits may be more profitable, he should so arrange that they take place regularly, and at stated times. With the accounts thus procured, and those collected in his personal visits, he will have material for a complete report at least once a year, to the Superior or Central Council, and afterwards to the Council-General, of the Works of the circumscription.

The President of a Council is the tie between the Conferences of the same circumscription.—The President of a Council should be a bond of union between all the Conferences of the same circumscription; by his visits and correspondence, he may easily maintain amongst them mutual good relations, and a spirit of union and concord, so important to the prosperity of the Society. This result will be more easily attained with Conferences in the same town; if rivalries exist, if coldness or divisions prevail amongst them, in consequence of inequality of influence or resources, he may soften asperities, remove all possible cause of misunderstanding, and re-unite all parties, by urging them to visit each other, pray together, and join in the practice of good works.

DUTIES OF THE PRESIDENT TOWARDS MEMBERS.

Relations of the President towards Members.— A President ought to be accessible to all his brother members, showing towards all the same kind and fraternal manner. We have already said that he is the soul of the work; he must also be its heart; between him and the members there should therefore, flow a current of Christian friendship, of which he ought to be the source; blending and combining the wills of all, and thus making of the Conference, as it were, one family.

In his words and actions he should demonstrate his love for his fellow members, and should teach them as far as lies in his power, to love one another; he should seize every occasion of uniting them in the Works; and in order to strengthen these ties he must have regard to similarity of age, character and position.

Maintaining concord amongst the members.— Jealousies, little as regards their comparative influence, sometimes cause coldness and disunion amongst the members; to re-establish concord, the President should give judicious advice and, adopting every measure of conciliation, show in himself an example of humility, condescension and mildness. If he has to suffer from the disagreeable temper or disposition of a member, he should not conduct himself towards that person in a cold or unfriendly manner; on the contrary, he should meet him with more cordiality than ever, even with marked attention; by this means he will do more for the general edification of the Conference for the good of the Works, and his own sanctification, than by giving way to a natural impulse of rebuking the member, even though rebuke should have been deserved.

To visit sick or afflicted Members.—This is a duty which a President's own heart will point out to him, and in which his feelings must be his guide; it is therefore only necessary to mention it. However, besides the ailments of the body, there are afflictions of the soul, which equally claim the fraternal attention of the President. Coldness, or want of zeal in the Works, carelessness, long absence from the Conference, or from the feasts of the Society—are symptoms which it is scarcely possible to mistake. As soon as a member shall have manifested these symptoms, the President must endeavour to assist this failing soul, and by kindness and delicate cares, by counsels of Christian tenderness, administered skilfully, and at proper times, and by the efforts of charitable friends, preserve it from a miserable fall.

Manner of receiving New Members, and general conduct of the President towards them.—To call on new members, whether they have come from another Conference, or have been recently admitted into the Society, to welcome them at the meetings, to make them acquainted with the other members, to take them amongst the poor, to initiate them in the works ; all these are important duties which a President must not fail to discharge, or, if he cannot himself fulfil them, he should be careful to depute some one in his place. It is of the utmost importance that new members should not, as sometimes happens, be forced to retire from a Conference because they are treated with coldness and reserve ; or that those who present themselves with letters of introduction from other Conferences should remain unnoticed ; on the contrary, their good will and experience in our works should be turned to account.

Form of Letters of Introduction.—The letters of introduction of which we have spoken, either serve to introduce and procure a welcome for a member who merely desires to visit a Conference, or they become for him a title of admission, when he wishes to pass from one Conference to another. It may well be supposed, however, that the style must be different in each case : each should be personal, special, and addressed to the President ; but that intended to procure the admission of a member should contain more particulars, and be drawn up in a form which would render it impossible for him to use it as a certificate for any other purpose.

A President should not too readily write such a letter; he should first ask himself, if the member who requires it fulfils all the conditions necessary for continuing in the Society. If serious reasons cause him to refuse the letter, the President will acquaint the applicant, in a kind and charitable manner, with the motives of his refusal; by so proceeding he may induce a salutary change in the member himself; at all events he will have discharged his duty by guarding the interests of the Society—which owes its prosperity and even its existence, to the proper selection of members.

No Certificate or Diploma to be given.—Under no circumstances should a President give a certificate to a member, on the ground that he has been for a shorter or longer time connected with the Conference; any attestation of this kind, made in a general form, might give rise to serious abuses; in fact, persons who had formerly belonged to a Conference, but had ceased to take part in its works, have been known to turn to improper uses, certificates which they had thus received. For similar reasons, the President should oppose the custom of giving diplomas, even if asked for merely as a pious souvenir, to members who are actually taking part in the works of the Conference. If we enter the Society, not for worldly reasons, but for our own good, what is the use of having a certificate that we are or have been members of it?

Letters of introduction given to young persons going to large towns.—With regard to young persons already members of the Society, and whose business or studies call them to large towns where there are Conferences, the President should not wait for them to solicit letters of introduction; he should rather anticipate their wishes, in order to prepare for them means of perseverance, with which they might not perhaps think of providing themselves, and which they may greatly need in the tumult of their new sphere of life. He might even propose to give such letters to young persons, who do not belong to the Conference, but are in every way eligible as members, and who for similar reasons change their residence.

Letters of recommendation given to the poor.— The observations already made about letters of introduction given to members, may, with still greater force, be applied to letters of recommendation given to the poor, to workmen, and apprentices going from one place to another. It is of far greater importance that these letters should be personal and *special;* they should not be put in the form of certificates, lest they become, in the hands of unscrupulous persons, means for working on the confiding charity of the Conferences where they might be presented.

Expulsion of a member.—The expulsion of an unworthy member from a Conference, is, undoubtedly, the most painful duty which a President can be called on to discharge. Thanks be to God, occasions for the exercise of this duty are very rare; in general, the member, feeling his own unworthiness, makes a timely retreat, and the President has then only to ratify his step, by erasing his name from the roll of the Conference. If, however, he persist in remaining, this painful act of severity will unfortunately become necessary. Before taking so extreme a measure, the President should convince himself of the unworthiness of the member, by a profound and attentive examination of his conduct, and by numerous, precise, but discreet inquiries; then, having arrived at a well-grounded conviction, and prepared himself by prayer to unite firmness with charity and mildness, he should seek the member, and urge and conjure him to hand in his resignation, in order to prevent the scandal of an expulsion; but if—as is very unlikely—he should not succeed, he will pronounce the sentence of expulsion, after taking the advice of the Board of his Conference, and of the Particular Council. In making this sentence known to the offender, he will be careful to soften the rigour of the measure by the charitable manner in which it is conveyed, and thus blend the indulgence of the Christian with the just severity of the President.

A President is not required to interest himself in the temporal concerns of Members.—We have said that a President should love his brother members. This must be specially understood with reference to their spiritual interests. It is not expected that he should take any part in the success of their worldly affairs, or in the promotion of their temporal interests. From the moment that personal services rendered by him to members gave rise to the idea that, in addition to opportunities for exercising charity towards the poor, means would be afforded them also for advancing in the world—from that moment the Conferences would be besieged by persons, who would come professedly to shed tears over the wants of the poor, but in reality to forward their own personal objects, by seeking patronage, support and influence for their worldly advancement, in the practice of our works. A President should invariably decline to exercise his influence when solicited for it under such circumstances. He should discountenance all applications and expectations of the kind, whether addressed to or reposed in himself or any other member of the Society.

The Council-General, the other Councils, or the Conferences ought not to occupy themselves with the temporal concerns of Members.—It may here be repeated that neither the Council-General nor the other Councils or Conferences to which members are too often recommended, for places or promotion, or for the arrangement of personal affairs, can or ought to attend to these recommendations. We should not be expected to render such services. Our efforts and aspirations tend to a higher object; if men of influence or wealth are to be found in our ranks, they are engaged in the cause of the poor, and the general edification, not for the purpose of rendering personal services; therefore, they owe to their brother members nothing more than friendly counsel and good example.

DUTIES WITH REGARD TO THE CLERGY.

We should consider the clergy as the guardian angels of our Conferences, who alone can keep us in the way of Christian charity. Veneration, devotedness, attachment, and confidence, should, at all times and under all circumstances, inspire and regulate our intercourse with the clergy; in this matter Presidents are especially interested.

To confer on Clergymen the title of President of Honour or Member of Honour.—It often happens that zealous clergymen wish to take part in our works; it is then customary to confer on them the title of *members of honour*, which places them above *honorary* or *active members*. It would be well to offer this title to the various clergymen of the parish, and that of *president of honour* to the parish priest or bishop of the diocese, according to localities and circumstances.

Presence of the Clergy at ordinary or at General Meetings.—The presence of clergymen at our meetings entails certain obligations which it is important to notice. We should distinguish between their habitual presence at Conferences, and their presence at general or extraordinary meetings. In the latter case, every honour should be shown to those clergymen, especially if they be dignitaries or Princes of the Church, who, by their presence, shed lustre on these assemblies; the President then only regulates the working of the meeting, and always holds the second rank. But at the Conference meetings, when a clergyman is present who is in the habit of attending, it is right to give him a place of honour, to show him regard and respect, and to ask him to recite the prayers ; the entire direction of the business remains, however, with the President.

To demand permission to introduce new works.— If a Conference wish to introduce new and important works into a Parish, the President should first obtain the consent of the ecclesiastical authorities ; and even when he seeks not for their direct and efficient aid, he should, at least be assured of their tacit approval.

For the various works of piety or sanctification, which nearly always take place in the churches, and especially for charity sermons and retreats, this approbation should, of course, be *formally* obtained. In these matters we must not so far presume on our lengthened and constant experience of the good will of the parish priest, as to omit applying to him for his formal sanction ; he is, in fact, the sole judge of the conditions on which he ought to take part in our works.

Duties with regard to Clergymen who preach for the benefit of our Works.—When a priest is asked by a Conference to preach a charity sermon, or to give a retreat in a diocese in which he is a stranger, it is necessary to inform the bishop of the diocese, and to obtain his permission.

When a preacher comes thus to assist our works by his eloquence, it is the duty of the President to meet him, either in person, or by deputy, show him every attention, and spare him, during the time of his sojourn, those many cares and inconveniences in seeking a lodging and providing for his other wants, which it would be unbecoming to place upon him. Accompanied, if possible, by some of the members, he should wait upon the preacher to return him thanks in the name of the Conference; he should also express the gratitude of the Conference to the parish priest, for his share in the good work.

Forms of Politeness to be observed towards the Clergy.—Various circumstances impose upon a President the observance of certain forms of politeness to priests; thus, when he first becomes President, at the new year, on different feast days, or when a new parish priest or bishop is appointed, he should pay his respects to the head of the parish, and still more to the head of the diocese, if resident in town. In this matter he will be guided by the sentiments already spoken of, which have their source in the profound veneration which the priestly character should inspire in every Christian. With this idea always before him, the President will seek every opportunity to make the Conference useful or acceptable to the bishop or parish priest in the organization and duties of diocesan and parochial works, or even in the solemnities and ceremonies of the Church; guarding himself, however, from indiscretions consequent upon excessive zeal, and taking into consideration local circumstances.

Conduct of the President when divisions or conflicts arise in the diocese or parish.—If dissensions exist in a parish or diocese, or if conflicts arise, the President should take care that none of the agitation or excitement resulting therefrom find its way into the Conference. He should not permit the subject to be mentioned, or even alluded to during the meetings; in his Presidential capacity he should keep a great reserve outside the Conference, avoiding in his acts or words all that might be misconstrued into want of regard or respect for the sacred character of a priest, and which might compromise the work over which he presides.

In such circumstances (always delicate and painful), as well as upon all other occasions, the sure way of avoiding error is to be penetrated with sincere humility, founded on the consciousness of our own nothingness. If this sentiment be connected in our souls with a high esteem and profound respect for the priesthood, and especially a cordial love for our pastors who continue in our regard the ministry of Jesus Christ, it is, and ever will be impossible for us either to say or do anything likely to hurt the feelings of our fathers and guides in the way of salvation.

DUTIES OF PRESIDENTS WITH REGARD TO THE CIVIL AUTHORITIES.

The President of a Conference, or of a Council is the representative and the recognized organ of his brother members with regard to the civil authorities. His relations with the latter, whether they be Protestant or Catholic, favorable or unfavorable to the works of the Society, should therefore be conducted in the same spirit of deference and conciliation. All Christians, but especially those engaged in charitable works, should set the example of paying due respect to constituted authority.

Assistance to be given by the Conference to the local Authorities in the administration of Charity.—When the accidental or unforeseen increase of poverty in a locality requires from the local authorities, an increase of assistance beyond the resources at their command, they are often obliged to have recourse to the Conferences, and to look to them for aid. This appeal should always be responded to; it would even be desirable that the President, anticipating such wants and wishes, should come forward to offer his assistance and that of his brother members whenever possible. By this foresight and these charitable attentions, he will the better succeed in destroying prejudices, gaining sympathy, and opening a more extended sphere for our works.

Conduct with regard to works established by the local Authorities.—Where works established or directed by local authorities already exist, the establishment of Conferences is sometimes regarded as injurious; the best means of overcoming this unfortunate prejudice is to watch for every opportunity of serving such works, and carefully to avoid everything that could have even the appearance of supplanting or injuring them in any manner. Acting upon this advice, when appeals are made for charitable purposes in general, a President should manifest great reserve and discretion. At such a time, more than at any other, the Conferences might create jealousy, if they did not observe great prudence ; besides, as their special duty is to watch over the moral and religious improvement of the poor, depending for success rather upon great personal devotedness than upon large resources, they ought to content themselves with merely gleaning, where other works reap an abundant harvest.

Difficulties with the local authorities.—Should difficulties arise in connection with the local authorities,—as, for example, if concessions be demanded which are incompatible with the spirit and rules of the Society,—the President, to avoid publicity, should confer with his Board, and not mention the matter to the Conference ; or he may take in private, the opinions of a few prudent members, or enlightened clergymen, and if necessary, refer to the Council of the circumscription. In every case he should avoid public demonstrations, and endeavour, through the medium of prudent and influential persons, well-disposed towards the Society, as well as by respectful and conciliatory representations, to soften difficulties and remove misunderstandings, which may, for the most part, be attributed to ignorance of the objects and organization of our Society.

Formal observances to be fulfilled.—The difficulties of which we have spoken will become rare if we take care to observe the formalities and rules which, according to the customs of various countries, regulate works of benevolence. The diversity of customs prevailing in different countries where our Society is established, makes it impossible to give precise details. It is sufficient to lay down this general rule ; *our Society should, in all places, show an example of respect for the law, and comport itself with the utmost deference towards the civil powers.*

DUTIES OF PRESIDENTS WITH REGARD TO OTHER CHARITABLE SOCIETIES.

Relations and Communications with other Works of Charity.—We find in the rules that " one of the vices most opposed to charity and Christian humility is envy. . . We should see without jealousy our Christian friends devoting themselves to other good works, and other societies doing God's work in their own manner, and independently of us. . . . We should ever believe that other societies obtain larger and better results than our own."

These are the dispositions which a President should possess, and which he should excite in the hearts of his brother members towards all other charitable societies. Far from placing himself in rivalry with them, he should contribute, as much as possible, to their prosperity and progress, without, however, employing the name or resources of his own Society, for he is the guardian of that name, and cannot compromise it in works for which he is not responsible ; he is the guardian of those resources, and must not employ them for any other object than that for which they have been collected. He should not refuse to enter into communication with these societies; but on the contrary, seek every occasion of having friendly understanding with them for the good of the poor, and better distribution of the assistance given.

Works performed by Associations of Ladies.— There are, in many localities, associations of ladies, occupied with the same works as ourselves; there are even some who have adopted the rules, the organization, and the very name of our Society, though they cannot, in any case, become aggregated to it. We should profit by their existence to induce them to visit poor families, consisting almost entirely of young women or girls, where the members of a Conference could not perhaps with propriety visit. For this end, the President will do well to establish friendly relations with these associations.

Duties towards Benefactresses who solicit contributions.—We must here say a word on the duties of the President towards those charitable ladies who co-operate in our works, by accepting the frequently ungrateful task of procuring resources by charity sermons, concerts, bazaars, &c. By his personal attentions, or those of some other member, he should relieve them of as much trouble as possible. Above all, he should not neglect, when their mission is ended, to express to them the gratitude of the Conference, which they have so kindly served.

It is said that politeness is one of the forms of charity; by these marks of attention, this scrupulous respect for the outward observances of courtesy, and particularly by disinterested relations with other charitable societies, we shall truly follow the example of our holy patron, and become men of many works and not of one work alone.

DUTIES OF PRESIDENTS TOWARDS THE PUBLIC.

Not to multiply appeals to public charity.—In the first rank of these duties is the discretion and prudence which a President should show in appealing to public charity in favour of the Society. Whatever be the importance or utility of the object, it is necessary that he restrain that too general tendency in Conferences to seek elsewhere, resources which may not readily be at hand amongst themselves. These multiplied appeals weary the good will of charitable persons, and relax the zeal of members, by habituating them to reckon more on others than on themselves.

The President should be sociable.—Another duty which the President owes to the works, as promoting their interest and well-being, is not to live too much isolated, but to keep up and extend those social relations which may prove useful to the Society. A certain degree of sociability is allied even to the most austere Christian virtue; there is no more effectual way of promoting the cause of virtue and religion than by being always amiable and agreeable. In this manner he will the better succeed in overcoming, where they exist, those unfortunate prejudices which too often establish a line of demarcation between men holding different positions in the social scale, but who should be united by the same Christian spirit. By showing himself equally affable, kind and accessible to all, he will contribute much to do away with unhappy jealousies which hinder the progress of good works.

The President has no right to any position or privilege above the rest of the public.—The President has duties to fulfil towards the public, but he has no right to assume any position or prerogative above others. Thus, in public solemnities or religious ceremonies, he is not to lay claim to any distinction, or to seek for any reserved place; he should even consider such honours as incompatible with the spirit of humility, which ought to form the ground-work of our Society. When the interests of the poor, or the works of the Society are not in question, he should not, for the same reason, make an ostentatious display of his title of President, in letters or recommendations addressed to persons who do not belong to the Conferences. The circumstance of his being President confers on him no other privilege than that of having the first and largest share in works which are pleasing to God.

To speak with humility of the works of the Society.—A President should always observe the precepts of humility, not only with regard to himself, but also with regard to his Conference and to the whole Society. If obliged to speak of them in public, he should do so in a brief manner, and in simple and modest terms; he should refrain from eulogizing in public his brother members either living or dead; praise does not add to the good they have done, but inflicts a severe blow on the spirit of humility. In making reports, he should avoid with care everything resembling a boast of the works, or of the members.

To avoid too great publicity.—A President must remember that publicity is perilous to the works, which require the sympathy, but not the applause of men, and to which the spirit of humility is as essential as the spirit of charity. He should particularly and strenuously oppose publication in the newspapers. They are an arena into which we cannot enter without being exposed to attacks utterly unsuitable to a work of peace and charity like ours.

To keep politics out of the Conference.—If the President be careful to keep *polemics* out of his Conference, he should guard still more from the introduction of *politics*; he cannot be too vigilant in preventing our Society from being even suspected of mixing in politics. Saint Vincent of Paul himself said "that those who profess to be ministers of charity, should not broach amongst themselves those worldly matters which cause so many dissensions amongst men." The President should, then, expel from the meetings every approach to politics, as well in the conversations which precede, as in those which follow the business; whether the general interests of the country, or those of the locality only be in question, let him remember that if politics be introduced, the piece of bread which we give to the poor will be changed into stone, and the Society of Saint Vincent of Paul soon be destroyed.

Personal conduct of the President in political matters.—As to the personal conduct of the President in political matters, he should so regulate it externally that his quality of President should be always distinct from that of citizen, particularly in those circumstances in which malevolent minds might injure our works. It would certainly be unjust to make the Society responsible for the opinions of its members; but this injustice may be easily committed, if the members are not guarded in the expression of their ideas and convictions; a President cannot, therefore, without jeopardising the Society, depart from the rules of moderation and discretion in all his acts, words, or writings with regard to political matters. He may, it is true, in circumstances of unusual gravity, have to choose between the President and the politician, and may find that one of these positions clashes with the other; he should then examine himself before God and his conscience, and choose that side on which he can do most good. The best course for a Christian to follow is that which tends to the greater glory of God and his own sanctification.

PERSONAL DUTIES OF THE PRESIDENT.

The President should examine himself with regard to the supervision of the Works.—A religious man makes each day an examination of his acts, and of his thoughts, with regard to his spiritual advancement. In the same manner a President requires to examine himself frequently in the presence of God, with regard to his direction of the works, at the head of which he is placed. He should ask himself if he does all that he ought to do in this respect, or all that he can do; if, under his management, they prosper and multiply, or, on the contrary, remain stationary, or go to decay.

A President should resign if he finds that he is an obstacle to the success of the Works.—If a President should discover that he does not sufficiently unite all the qualities of a good President—if he should perceive that the Conference is declining, that his age, his character, his occupations, or his personal circumstances, are obstacles to the prosperity or progress of the works; if, moreover, he be convinced that another person is better suited for the post; if he be confirmed in this idea by the opinions of enlightened persons, then he should not hesitate to resign; but this should be accomplished without noise or disturbance to the Conference, at the most opportune moment, and only after a worthy successor has been chosen. The President owes this sacrifice to the interests of the Conference, and he would not be its true friend if he could refuse it. Devotion to the Society has been carried to so great an extent by some Presidents that they have not hesitated to sacrifice a position and advantages which they thought likely to interfere with it. These examples should teach us that if we are not prepared to sacrifice ourselves for the interests of the society, we ought at least not to sacrifice the Society to our own convenience.

He should distrust his own humility when examining himself on his duties.—In his self-examination he should guard against excessive humility or too great timidity. Discouragement, fatigue and indolence, sometimes arm us with a false severity against ourselves, and this proceeds from our self-love. In such a case, before arriving at a final resolution, a President should appeal from his own judgment to the opinions of enlightened persons; for in fact, we see clearly our faults or imperfections only through the eyes of others.

Advantages of this examination in the fulfilment of his duties as President.—Whatever be the result of this examination, whether the President discover that he must seek for a successor, or decide upon continuing to preside over the Conference, these reflections on his direction of the works, on their requirements, on their progress or decline, will be useful in the highest degree. A zealous and active President should frequently turn his thoughts to this subject. He will certainly make useful resolutions, and imbibe fresh ardor in the service of God and the poor.

These little instructions will facilitate for Presidents this species of examination of conscience with regard to the works, by tracing the paths they should follow; and, at the same time help them to ascertain the points on which they have gone astray. They are, therefore earnestly advised frequently and attentively to peruse these pages, which, though somewhat prolix, are yet not complete; experience and reflection will, however, point out all that is wanting, and give the readers opportunities of drawing from their own hearts many valuable inspirations. In conclusion, let all seriously reflect on this maxim of Saint Vincent of Paul, which is a perfect summary of the foregoing pages.

"*The defects which are found in an association, generally arise from the negligence of him who presides over it. In the same manner the good conduct of the members depends on the regularity of their President, and on the prudence and wisdom of his government.*"

PRAYERS

AT THE

Beginning and end of the Meetings,

Prayers at the opening of Meetings.

IN the name of the Father, and of the Son, and of the Holy Ghost, Amen.

Come, O Holy Ghost, fill the hearts of thy faithful, and kindle in them the fire of Thy love.

V. Send forth Thy Spirit, and they shall be regenerated.

R. And Thou wilt renew the face of the earth.

Let us pray.

O GOD, who, by the light of the Holy Ghost, didst instruct the hearts of the faithful; grant that by the same Spirit we may be truly wise, and ever enjoy His consolation, through Jesus Christ our Lord.

R. Amen.
V. Saint Vincent of Paul.
R. Pray for us.

In the name, &c.

Prayers at the close of Meetings.

In the name, &c.

Let us pray.

MOST Gracious Jesus, who didst raise up in the Church blessed Vincent for an apostle of Thy most ardent charity, pour forth upon Thy servants that same fervour of Charity, that for the love of Thee, they may with a most ready heart bestow their goods upon the poor, and spend themselves for their souls. Who with God the Father livest and reignest in the unity of the Holy Ghost, one God, world without end.
R. Amen.

For Benefactors.

VOUCHSAFE, we beseech Thee, Thy grace to the benefactors of the poor, most tender Jesus, who hast promised a hundred fold and a heavenly kingdom to them that do works of mercy in Thy name.
R. Amen.

We fly to Thy patronage, O Holy Mother of God; despise not our petitions in our necessities, but deliver us from all dangers, O ever glorious and blessed Virgin.
R. Amen.

And may the souls of the faithful through the mercy of God rest in peace.
R. Amen.

Let us pray.

WE give Thee thanks, O Lord, for the manifold blessings and favours which Thou hast hitherto deigned to bestow on the Society of Thy holy servant, Vincent of Paul.

And now, we beseech of Thee a continuance of those blessings for that Society which is so dear to us all, for each of our Conferences, and in particular for that of which we are members. Grant, we beseech Thee, that it may be strengthened, increased, and perpetuated with its primitive spirit of piety, simplicity and fraternal union, so that its labours being utterly freed from all worldly interest, it may become still more productive of heavenly fruit.

Thou knowest, O Lord, the many wants, both spiritual and temporal, that press on the poor families helped by our scanty service. Thou knowest our own many wants. Have mercy upon us, and let all experience the effects of Thine infinite mercy.

More particularly do we implore Thee, O Most Gracious Lord, to assist those among our brethren who may be at this moment undergoing trials of any kind. Grant, we beseech Thee, that they may never fail in obtaining that fortitude, prudence, peace, and hope which come from above, and that their trials as well as our own, being undergone with patience and resignation, may be made agreeable to Thee and bring forth fruit unto salvation.

Finally, we pour forth our supplications to Thee, O Lord, that through the merits of our

Lord Jesus Christ, and the special intercession of Blessed Mary and Holy Saint Vincent, our Patron, Thou wouldst grant that the poor families we have in charge, our relations, friends, and brethren, when released from the bonds of this our mortal state, be partakers with us of Thy Kingdom. Amen.

Prayer that may be recited by a Member before leaving home to visit the poor.

O Almighty God, direct our actions according to Thy divine will, that in the name of Thy beloved Son we may abound in good works.

Prevent, we beseech Thee, O Lord, our actions by Thy holy inspirations, and carry them on by Thy gracious assistance, that every prayer and work of ours may always begin from Thee, and by Thee be happily ended. Through Jesus Christ, Thy Son, &c. Amen.

THE HYMN "VENI CREATOR."

To be recited pending the election of a President.

COME Holy Ghost, Creator come,
   From Thy bright heavenly throne ;
Come, take possession of our souls,
   And make them all Thine own.

Thou who art call'd the Paraclete,
   Best gift of God above ;
The living spring, the living fire,
   Sweet unction and true love.

Thou who art seven-fold in Thy grace,
    Finger of God's right hand ;
His promise, teaching little ones
    To speak and understand.

O ! guide our minds with Thy blest light,
    With love our hearts inflame ;
And with Thy strength, which ne'er decays,
    Confirm our mortal frame.

Far from us drive our hellish foe,
    True peace unto us bring ;
And through all perils lead us safe,
    Beneath Thy sacred wing.

Through Thee may we the Father know,
    Through Thee th' eternal Son.
And Thee, the Spirit of them both,
    Thrice blessed Three in One.

All glory to the Father be,
    With his co-equal Son,
The like to Thee great Paraclete,
    Till time itself is done.   Amen.

PSALM CXXIX.—DE PROFUNDIS.

To be recited on the death of an active Member, Honorary Member, or Benefactor ; likewise of a person visited, if requested so to do.

OUT of the depths I have cried to Thee, O Lord ; Lord hear my voice.

    Let Thine ears be attentive to the voice of my supplication.

If Thou wilt observe iniquities, O Lord; Lord, who shall endure it?

Because with Thee there is propitiation; and by reason of Thy law I have waited for Thee, O Lord.

My soul hath relied on His word; my soul hath hoped in the Lord.

From the morning watch, even until night, let Israel hope in the Lord.

Because with the Lord there is mercy, and with Him plentiful redemption.

And he shall redeem Israel from all his iniquities.

V. Eternal rest give to them, O Lord.

R. And let perpetual light shine upon them.

Let us pray.

TO Thee, O Lord, we commend the soul of Thy servant N........., that being dead to the world, he (*or* she) may live to Thee; and whatever sins he (*or* she) may have committed through human frailty, do Thou, of Thy most merciful goodness, forgive, through Christ our Lord. Amen.

May he (*or* she) rest in peace.

R. Amen.

Let us pray.

GRANT, O God, that while we here lament the departure of this Thy servant, we may always remember that we are most certainly to follow him (*or* her). Give us grace to prepare for that last hour by a good life, that we may not be surprised by a sudden and unprovided death, but be ever watching, that when Thou shalt call, we may with the bridegroom enter into eternal glory. Through Jesus Christ our Lord.

R. Amen.

V. May the Divine assistance remain always with us.

R. Amen.

V. And may the souls of the faithful departed, through the mercy of God, rest in peace.

R. Amen.

Superior Council of Canada.

ARTICLE I.

All the Conferences of Canada are governed by a Superior Council, established in conformity to the dispositions of the Brief of His Holiness Pope Gregory XVI, dated 10th January, 1845. Its seat is at Quebec, and its title, the Superior Council of Canada.

This Council represents in Canada, the General Council of Paris, which is the head of the whole Society. The Superior Council has the direction of all the Councils and Conferences now established, or hereafter to be formed, in Canada. It maintains in this country the Unity and Spirit of the Society. It is the medium of correspondence between the Councils and Conferences of Canada, and the General Council.

ARTICLE II.

The Superior Council is composed of a President, one or more Vice-Presidents, one Secretary, one Treasurer, one or more Vice-Secretaries, or Vice-Treasurers, and several Councillors.

ARTICLE III.

The first election of the President of the Superior Council is made by all the Conferences.

ARTICLE IV.

When there is occasion to elect a new President of the Superior Council, the Council is summoned by the Vice-President. This meeting which is preparatory, is to consider of a fit person to fill that office, and the retiring President is requested to indicate the person whom he believes best qualified. When one or more names have been agreed upon, the Council adjourns for about two months. In the interval, a statement of the proceedings of this first meeting is furnished to the Presidents of the Particular Councils, who consult their Colleagues ; and to the Presidents of the Conferences who take the sense of their respective Boards or even of their Conferences ; each of them forthwith transmits the result of these deliberations to the Superior Council, which thereupon closes the election, and enters on its minutes an exact and detailed statement of the proceedings. Pending the election, all the members of the Society, either privately or at their meetings, offer up to God a special prayer—the *Veni Creator*—that His spirit may enlighten them and guide their choice.

ARTICLE V.

The Officers and Members of the Superior

Council are appointed by the President thereof, with the advice of the Council.

ARTICLE VI.

The President of the Superior Council presides at all the General Meetings of the Quebec Conferences, and, also, at all the meetings of the Superior Council. He summons all extraordinary meetings. In case of his absence, he appoints a Vice-President, or, if necessary, some other member of the Council, to preside in his stead.

ARTICLE VII.

The Secretary of the Superior Council keeps a Register of the names, surnames, callings, residences, and dates of reception, of the members of the Quebec Conferences, and also, of the members of the Boards of the different Councils and Conferences throughout Canada, together with the places, days, and hours of their meetings. He keeps minutes of the meetings of the Superior Council and of the General Meetings. He prepares the annual report of the labours of the Society and transmits it to the General Council. He is charged, under the direction of the President, with the correspondence with the Presidents or Secretaries of the different Councils or Conferences, and with the General Council. He is the Custodian of the Archives of the Society in Canada.

ARTICLE VIII.

The Treasurer holds the funds, takes note of the receipts and expenditure, and renders an account thereof to the Superior Council.

ARTICLE IX.

Two members of the Superior Council are appointed by the President to preside at the meetings of the Irish and French Councils of Quebec, should he be unable to perform that duty in person.

ARTICLE X.

The President of the Superior Council appoints the Presidents and Vice-Presidents of the Conferences and Special Works of Quebec, and also, the Boards of the two Councils in that city ; in these appointments he consults the Particular Councils.

ARTICLE XI.

The funds of the Superior Council are supplied by extraordinary gifts made to the Society, by the collections at the General Meetings, and by the annual offerings of each Conference or of each Particular Council in Canada towards covering the general expenses of the Society.

ARTICLE XII.

When a Conference or a Council is about to be formed in Canada, the Superior Council, enquires into the propriety of recommending to the General Council in Paris its aggregation. This aggregation can be pronounced only on the recommendation of the Superior Council; and when the Superior Council deems it expedient to dissolve a Conference or a Council, it refers that matter likewise, to the General Council.

ARTICLE XIII.

The Superior Council directs by correspondence, or by circulars from the President, all the details of the administration of the Conferences of Canada; under the guidance of the General Council, it also superintends the execution of the Regulations in all questions that concern the Society at large or that are of an important nature.

ARTICLE XIV.

When at Paris, the President of the Superior Council of Canada, assists and takes part in the meetings of the General Council, of which he is a member *ex officio*.

AN EASY METHOD

OF ATTENDING

HOLY MASS WITH PROFIT.

By the Blessed Leonard of Port-Maurice.

A Prayer of most humble devotion to the Holy Spirit, to be offered before hearing Holy Mass, in order to implore His aid.

Come, O Holy Spirit, and with Thy most holy grace gather together, I beseech of Thee, all the faculties and all the affections of my soul, so that, with devout attention, and with my whole heart, I may be able to attend this Holy Mass, and obtain thereby those benefits for which, albeit unworthy, I ardently hope, to the greater glory of God, and the benefit of my own soul, through the goodness and compassion of the same, my Lord and God. Amen.

Prayer while the Priest says the Confiteor.

O my most loving Saviour, Who when weighed down with faintness and grief of heart, in the garden of Gethsemani, didst turn in fervent prayer to the Eternal Father, while the drops of

Thy bloody sweat ran down profusely to the ground; grant me the grace that, in memory of Thy most holy passion, I may, at least, shed abundant tears of grief and contrition, as Thou, Thy bloody sweat of agony, that night. Amen.

Prayer when the Priest begins the Introit.

O my most benign and gentle Saviour, Who when led like a malefactor before Annas, didst receive from the fierce Jews those cruel blows, grant that, in imitation of Thee, I also may receive with willingness the affronts of mine enemies, and bear up under all the troubles and temptations of this treacherous world. Amen.

Prayer while the Priest repeats the Kyrie Eleison.

O my Lord Jesus Christ, Who in the house of Caiphas wast three times basely denied by Peter, chief of Thine Apostles; I humbly pray Thee, make me ever to shun wicked companions, so that I may never, by following them, and through mine own grievous sinfulness and imperfection, be led away from Thee and Thine infinite goodness. Amen.

Prayer while the Priest reads the Epistle.

O my most compassionate Saviour, Who being conducted to Pilate's house by the Jews, with every kind of outrage, wast unjustly accused by false witnesses in his presence: teach me, I pray Thee, to fly all the snares of the wicked;

and enable me, amid the constant practice of good works, ever sincerely and openly to profess Thy Holy Catholic Faith, till the latest moment of my life. Amen.

Prayer while the Priest reads the Gospel.

O my most merciful Lord, Who when sent back by Herod to Pilate, wast the occasion of their reconciliation, grant to me such strength that I may never fear the devices of the wicked, but rather obtain from persecution and trials, such benefit, that even in the midst of them, my heart may never be troubled, but ever grow more and more conformed, in and by all things, to Thy most Holy will. Amen.

Prayer while the Priest offers the Sacrifice.

My Lord Jesus Christ, Who to satisfy the justice of Thine Eternal Father for my sins, didst freely choose to be bound to the column, and under so many stripes to scatter Thy most precious blood; grant me grace to cleanse my soul of the hideous stains of sin in those ruddy streams, so that I may offer it all fresh and pure in union with Thy merits to the Eternal Father. Amen.

Prayer while the Priest washes his fingers.

O my most compassionate Saviour, O Son of the Living God, Who when declared innocent by Pilate Thy judge, didst patiently bear the tumult and the eager cries of the Jews, in their bitter malice against Thee; grant me the grace to lead a life truly innocent amid the stormy waves of this world, and to present only the resistance of patient charity to the outrages and attacks of enemies. Amen.

Prayer while the Priest says the Preface.

O my most sweet and gentle Saviour, Who didst receive from Pilate the unjust sentence to die ignominiously on the cross, grant me the grace, that when I shall arrive at the last hour of my life, I may, through love of Thee, feel no fear when my sentence of death, however painful, has at last to be put in force; but that I may sigh out my soul in the embrace of Thy most sacred arms. Amen.

Prayer while the Priest prays for the Living.

O my most compassionate Saviour, Who didst will, for the redemption of the world, to carry the heavy cross upon Thy shoulders, even to Mount Calvary, grant me the grace, that, following Thine example, I may willingly embrace the cross of the mortifications and trials of this world, and bear it patiently, for love of Thee, even until death. Amen.

Prayer while the Priest elevates the Host.

O my most merciful Saviour, Who after being shamefully nailed to the cross by the hands of wicked men, wast lifted up from the ground upon it; uplift, I beseech Thee, by the excess of Thine infinite compassion, my poor heart above all earthly passions and cares, so as to give my mind to nothing but thoughts of Thy most holy Passion, of my own death, and of the eternal things of heaven. Amen.

Prayer while the Priest elevates the Chalice.

My Lord Jesus Christ, Who didst will that the true fountain of all graces should be Thy Blood gushing over us from Thy most sacred wounds, cause me always, when suddenly assailed by evil thoughts, to have recourse to the power and efficacy of those most sacred wounds, and to draw from them my certain remedy, so as ever to rise victorious over temptation during my whole life. Amen.

Prayer to implore the gift of Divine Love.

Wound, O Lord, my soul with Thy holy love. Pierce my hard heart with Thy charity;—Sweet Jesus, by the mystery of Thy sacred Body, and by the five wounds through which Thy Blood was poured out for me, have mercy on my soul according to its needs. Receive me according to Thy word, and let not my hope be confounded.—Thou Who art all Merciful, take pity on me. Amen.

Prayer while the Priest intercedes for the Departed.

My most gracious Saviour, Who while fixed in anguish on the cross, didst pray to Thine

Eternal Father for the salvation of all the human race, even for those who crucified Thee; inflame my heart with the heavenly fire of a most ardent love, so that in all time coming, taught by Thine example, I may learn tenderly to love my neighbour, and do good even to mine enemies. Amen.

Prayer while the Priest recites the Our Father.

My Lord Jesus Christ, Who just before Thy death of most bitter anguish, didst recommend Thy Mother, the most Blessed Virgin, to Saint John, and then the same John to her; be pleased ever to accept my body and soul, so that by means of Thy most holy help, I may quickly advance in the way of the Spirit and of perfection. Amen.

Prayer while the Priest puts into the Chalice a portion of the Host.

O my most merciful Saviour, Who descending after death didst rejoice with Thy divine presence the poor expectant souls of the Patriarchs, cause, I beseech Thee, the virtue of Thy most precious blood, and of Thy most holy passion to descend upon all the souls suffering in purgatory, so that, freed from those dreadful pains, they may be admitted to enjoy the eternal glory of heaven. Amen.

Prayer while the Priest says the Agnus Dei.

My Lord Jesus Christ, since many of the Jews recognized their transgressions, and wept for their sins, at the cruel sight of Thy most bitter death, grant me grace, through the merits of that death, that I, too, may bitterly weep and lament for my sins. Amen.

Prayer while the Priest receives the Most Holy Communion.

My most gracious Lord, Who for the redemption of the whole human race, didst permit Thy most precious Body to be placed at burial in a new sepulchre, grant me the grace that my heart may be so made new as to be ready for Thee to enter therein. Amen.

Prayer while the Priest gives his Blessing to the People.

O my Lord, most loving and most worthy to be loved, Who while Thy disciples were all intently given to prayer, didst send down from heaven the Holy Spirit to console them; purify, I beseech Thee, my heart with Thy most holy grace, so that the Holy Spirit finding in it a pleasing abode, may dwell therein, and so enrich the poverty of my soul. Amen.

MASS OF THE FEAST
OF THE
Immaculate Conception of the B. V. Mary.

Eighth December.

INTROIT. *Isaias* ch. lxi.—I will greatly rejoice in the Lord, and my soul shall be joyful in my God, for He hath clothed me with the garments of salvation and with the robe of justice. He hath covered me as a bride adorned with her jewels. *Ps.* xxix. I will extol Thee, O Lord, for Thou hast upholden me and hast not made mine enemies to rejoice over me. *V.* Glory be to the Father, &c. *Repeat*, I will, &c., to *Ps.*

COLLECT.—O God, who by the Immaculate Conception of the Virgin, didst prepare for Thy Son a habitation worthy of Him; grant us, by her intercession, faithfully to keep our hearts and bodies immaculate for Thee, who didst preserve her from all stain. Through the same Jesus Christ, &c.

LESSON. *Proverbs* ch. viii.—The Lord possessed me in the beginning of His ways, before He made anything from the beginning; I was set up from eternity and of old, before the earth was made·—The depths were not as yet, and I was already conceived, neither had the fountains of water as yet sprung forth : the mountains with their huge bulk had not as yet been established : before the hills was I brought forth : He had not yet made the earth, nor the rivers, nor the poles of the world.—When He prepared the heavens I was present : when with a certain law and compass He enclosed the deep ; when He spanned the sky above and poised the fountains of waters : when He compassed the sea within its bounds, and set a law to the waters that they should not pass their limits ; when He balanced the foundations of the earth—I was with Him forming all things, and was delighted every day, playing before Him at all times ; playing in the world, and my delights were to be with the children of men.—Now therefore, ye children, hear me : blessed are they that keep my ways. Hear instruction and be wise, and refuse it not. Blessed is the man that heareth me and that watcheth daily at my gates, and waiteth at the posts of my doors. He that shall find me shall find life, and shall have salvation from the Lord.

GRADUAL. *Jud.* ch. xiii.—Blessed art thou O Virgin Mary by the Lord the Most High God, above all women upon the earth. *V.* Thou art the glory of Jerusalem, thou art the joy of Israel, thou art the honour of our people. *Alleluia, Alleluia. V. Cant.* iv. Thou art all fair, O Mary, and there is no original stain in thee. *Alleluia.*

GOSPEL. *Luke* ch. i.—At that time the Angel Gabriel was sent from God into a city of Galilee, called Nazareth, to a virgin espoused to a man, whose name was Joseph, of the house of David; and the virgin's name was Mary. And the Angel being come in, said unto her: Hail, full of grace, the Lord is with thee, blessed art thou among women.

OFFERTORY. *Luke* ch. i.—Hail Mary, full of grace, the Lord is with thee, blessed art thou among women. *Alleluia.*

SECRET.—Receive O Lord the Saving Victim which we offer to Thee, on the solemnity of the Immaculate Conception of the Blessed Virgin Mary; and grant that as we profess our faith in her exemption from every stain through Thy preventing grace, so through her intercession, may we be delivered from all our sins. Through our Lord Jesus Christ, &c.

COMMUNION.—Glorious things are said of thee, O Mary, because He that is mighty hath done great things unto thee.—

POST COMMUNION.—May the sacrament which we have received, O Lord our God, heal in us the wounds of that sin, from which, by a singular privilege, Thou didst preserve Immaculate the Conception of the Blessed Mary. Through our Lord Jesus Christ, &c.

PROPER MASS

OF

St. Vincent of Paul, Confessor.

Nineteenth July.

INTROIT. *Ps.* 91.—The just shall flourish like the palm tree ; he shall grow up like the cedar of Libanus ; planted in the house of the Lord, in the courts of the house of our God ; *Ps.* It is good to give praise to the Lord, and to sing to Thy name, O most High. *V.* Glory be to the Father, &c. *Repeat*, The just, &c.

COLLECT. O God, who didst strengthen blessed Vincent with apostolic power to preach the gospel to the poor, and advance the honour of the ecclesiastical order, grant, we beseech Thee, that as we venerate his merits of charity, so we may be instructed by the many examples of his virtues ; Through our Lord Jesus Christ Thy Son, &c.

EPISTLE. 1 *Cor.* iv., 9-15.—Brethren, we are made a spectacle to the world, and to angels, and to men ; we are fools for Christ's sake, but you are wise in Christ ; we are weak, but you are strong ; you are honourable, but we without honour. Even unto this hour we both hunger and thirst, and are naked, and are buffetted, and have no fixed abode, and we labour, working with our own hands. We are reviled, and we bless; we are persecuted, and we suffer it; we are blasphemed, and we entreat; we are made as the refuse of this world, the off-scouring of all, even until now. I write not these things to confound you; but I admonish you as my dearest children, in Christ Jesus our Lord.

GRADUAL. *Ps.* 36.—The mouth of the just shall meditate wisdom, and his tongue shall speak judgment. *V.* The law of his God is in his heart: and his steps shall not be supplanted. *Alleluia, alleluia.—Ps.* 111. Blessed is the man that feareth the Lord: he delights exceedingly in His commandments. *Alleluia.*

GOSPEL. *St. Luke,* x., 1–9. *At that time;* The Lord appointed also other seventy-two: and He sent them two and two before His face into every city and place whither He Himself was to come. And He said to them: The harvest indeed is great, but the labourers are few. Pray ye, therefore, the Lord of the harvest, that He send labourers into His harvest. Go: behold I send you as lambs among wolves. Carry neither purse, nor scrip, nor shoes; and salute no man by the way. Into whatsoever house you enter, first say, Peace be to this house. And if the son of peace be there, your peace shall rest upon him; but if not, it shall return to you. And in the same house remain, eating and drinking such things as they have. For the labourer is worthy of his hire. Remove not from house to house. And into what city soever you enter, and they receive you, eat such things as are set before you. And heal the sick that are therein, and say to them: The Kingdom of God is come nigh unto you.

OFFERTORY. *Ps.* 20.—In Thy strength, O Lord, the just shall joy, and in Thy salvation he shall rejoice exceedingly: Thou hast given him his heart's desire.

SECRET.—Grant we beseech Thee, Almighty God, that the oblation of our humility may be pleasing to Thee, in honour of Thy saints, and may also purify us in body and in mind; Through our Lord Jesus Christ, Thy Son, &c.

COMMUNION. *St. Matt.* 19.—Amen I say to you, that you who have left all things, and followed Me, shall receive a hundred fold, and possess life everlasting.

POST COMMUNION.—We beseech Thee, Almighty God, that we, who have received heavenly food, may, through the intercession of blessed Vincent, Thy Confessor, be protected by the same from all adversity; Through our Lord Jesus Christ, Thy Son, &c.

THE
Litany of St. Vincent of Paul.

Lord have mercy on us.
Christ, have mercy on us.
Lord, have mercy on us.
Jesus, hear us.
Jesus, graciously hear us.
God the Father of heaven, have mercy on us.
God the Son, Redeemer of the world, have mercy on us.
God the Holy Ghost, have mercy on us.
Holy Trinity, one God, have mercy on us.
Holy Mary, pray for us.

Holy Mary, mother of Christ, the Sovereign Priest,
St. Vincent, who from your infancy, walked in the presence of God,
St. Vincent, most benevolent to all,
St. Vincent, chaste and pure,
St. Vincent, watchful shepherd of the flocks intrusted to your care,
St. Vincent, who so faithfully preached the gospel to the poor,
St. Vincent, who brought your disciples to the practice of all good works.
St. Vincent, the glory of the priesthood,

} Pray for us.

St. Vincent, humble amidst the honours of the world,
St. Vincent, careful imitator of Jesus Christ,
St. Vincent, alleviator of human misery,
St. Vincent, refuge and comforter of the afflicted,
St. Vincent, feeder of the hungry,
St. Vincent, friend of the sick,
St. Vincent, father of orphans,
St. Vincent, refuge of purity and security of innocence,
St. Vincent, zealous seeker of wandering souls,
St. Vincent, restorer of the beauty of ecclesiastical discipline,
St. Vincent, like an angel at the altar,
St. Vincent, strong in holy obedience and faith,
St. Vincent, burning with zeal for the glory of God,

} Pray for us.

Lamb of God, who takest away the sins of the world.
Spare us, O Lord.
Lamb of God, &c.
Graciously hear us, O Lord.
Lamb of God, &c.
Have mercy on us.
V. He made Himself all to all.
R. Let us walk in His footsteps.

Let us pray.

O Jesus, meek and humble of heart! since humble souls only can give glory to Thy Holy Name, and the dwelling of Thy Glory will be forever shut against me, unless I become truly humble, grant me humility, which alone can merit Thy Grace and secure me a place in Thine eternal Kingdom. Pardon, O my God! the manifold sins which I have committed through pride, and grant me a contempt for myself, proportioned to the pride which has so far enslaved me, but which I now so sincerely detest. I beg this favour through the intercession of our Holy Father, St. Vincent, who was truly meek and humble. Amen.

ANOTHER

Litany of St. Vincent of Paul,

Designed especially for Members of the Society.

Lord, have mercy on us.
Christ, have mercy on us.
Lord, have mercy on us.
Christ, hear us. Christ, graciously hear us.
God the Father of heaven, have mercy on us.
God the Son, Redeemer of the world, have mercy on us.
God the Holy Ghost, have mercy on us.
Holy Trinity, one God, have mercy on us.
Holy Mary, pray for us.
St. Vincent of Paul, pray for us.
St. Vincent of Paul, endowed from your earliest youth with the wisdom of old age,
St. Vincent of Paul, full of mercy from your infancy,
St. Vincent of Paul, chosen from being a simple shepherd to feed the heritage of the Lord,
St. Vincent of Paul, free in slavery and chains,
St. Vincent of Paul, the just, living by faith,
St. Vincent of Paul, ever tranquil and secure on the firm anchor of Christian hope,
} Pray for us.

St. Vincent of Paul, ever burning with the fire of charity,
St. Vincent of Paul, truly simple, upright and fearing God,
St. Vincent of Paul, meek, and humble of heart, true disciple of Jesus Christ,
St. Vincent of Paul, perfectly mortified in the spirit and the flesh,
St. Vincent of Paul, ever animated by the spirit of Christ,
St. Vincent of Paul, truly zealous for the glory of God,
St. Vincent of Paul, ever burning for the conversion of souls,
St. Vincent of Paul, declared and implacable enemy of the world and its maxims,
St. Vincent of Paul, rich in the treasures of Christian poverty,
St. Vincent of Paul, angel of purity,
St. Vincent of Paul, man of obedience, ever speaking of victories,
St. Vincent of Paul, devoted from youth to the labours of charity,
St. Vincent of Paul, ever careful to shun even the appearance of evil,
St. Vincent of Paul, ever aspiring to the most perfect virtues,
St. Vincent of Paul, immovable as a rock in the stormy sea of the world,
St. Vincent of Paul, constant as the sun in the paths of true wisdom,
St. Vincent of Paul, most patient in the midst of adversity,
St. Vincent of Paul, meek and forbearing,

Pray for us.

St. Vincent of Paul, devoted child of the Roman Church,
St. Vincent of Paul, inviolably attached unto death to the chair of St. Peter,
St. Vincent of Paul, ever averse to new doctrines and profane innovations,
St. Vincent of Paul, destined by Providence to evangelize the poor,
St. Vincent of Paul, most tender father of the clergy,
St. Vincent of Paul, wise founder of the Congregation of the Mission,
St. Vincent of Paul, prudent institutor of the Sisters of Charity,
St. Vincent of Paul, lovingly anxious to form your own disciples to every good work,
St. Vincent of Paul, full of tenderness and generosity towards the poor,
St. Vincent of Paul, unwearied in prayer and in the ministry of the word,
St. Vincent of Paul, zealous imitator of the life and virtues of Christ,
St. Vincent of Paul, faithful unto the end.
St. Vincent of Paul, whose death was precious before the Lord,
St. Vincent of Paul, happy now in the eternal possession of truth and charity,
St. Vincent of Paul, our father, that we may, like faithful children, walk in thy footsteps,

} Pray for us.

Lamb of God, who takest away the sins of the world: Spare us, O Lord.
Lamb of God, who takest away the sins of the world: Graciously hear us, O Lord.

Lamb of God, who takest away the sins of the world : Have mercy on us.

V. The Lord led the just man through ways of equity.

R. And showed unto him the Kingdom of God.

Let us pray.

O God, who for the salvation of the poor and the sanctification of the clergy, didst form by Blessed Vincent, a new family in Thy Church ; grant, we beseech Thee, that animated with his spirit, we may ever love what he loved, and practice what he taught, through Christ our Lord. Amen.

Prayer to St. Vincent of Paul.

O glorious St. Vincent, whose highest ambition was to relieve the poor, to comfort the suffering, to instruct the ignorant, to bring sinners to a spirit of penance, and to plant the Gospel precepts of charity, humility, meekness, and simplicity in the hearts of the faithful,—we earnestly commend our Society to thy powerful patronage.—Obtain for us from God, through the merits of His Only Son, Our Lord and Saviour Jesus Christ, that while we endeavour to assist the helpless and the destitute, and to instruct them in that all saving science, that one thing needful, for which alone we have been placed in this world, we may treasure up in our own hearts the knowledge of it, and make it the constant practice of our lives and conduct.

Obtain for us especially, O great Saint, the grace of faithfully imitating thy fervent zeal and piety in this charitable work which we have undertaken for the honour and glory of God's most Holy Name, and for the eternal salvation of the poor of Jesus, His beloved Son; to the end that we also may hereafter participate in that plentiful redemption which He has purchased for us with His most precious Blood. Amen.

And may the souls of the faithful, through the mercy of God, rest in peace. Amen.

DEVOTIONS FOR COMMUNION.

Prayers Before Receiving the Blessed Sacrament.

An Act of Faith.

God of heaven and earth, and Saviour of mankind, Thou comest to me, and I shall have the happiness to receive Thee,—*The bread I shall give*, sayest Thou (John ch. 6), *is my flesh, for the life of the world.*—The Jews found this saying hard; but to me it is a word of truth and happiness. I receive it with faith and gratitude. Yes, O Lord, I firmly believe that it is Thou, Thyself, Whom I am going to receive:—Thou, Who born for my sake in a manger, wast pleased to die for me on a cross, and Who, now glorious in heaven, art however truly concealed under the mysterious veils of Thy holy sacrament.

Verily Thou art a hidden God, the God of Israel, the Saviour.—Isaias ch. 45.

I do believe Lord, help Thou mine unbelief.—Mark ch. 9.

An Act of Humility.

But how shall I dare approach to Thee, O God of holiness.—Thou art the Lord of lords, the King of kings;—and who am I but dust and ashes; a despicable worm of the earth, and what is worse, an ungrateful sinner, who has so often offended Thee.—O Lord, never shall I be worthy to eat Thy sacred flesh, and to feed on the bread of angels. Yet Thou invitest me; nay, Thou *commandest* me to come to Thee.— Jesus, meek and humble of heart; Jesus, Who didst not disdain to sit at table with Publicans and sinners,—since Thou callest me, I obey with humble submission, and say from my heart, with Thy Blessed Mother, *Behold* thy servant; *be it done to me according to Thy Word.*—Luke ch. 1.

O Lord, I am not worthy.—Matt. ch. 8.

A contrite and humble heart, O Lord, Thou wilt not despise.—Psalm 50.

An Act of Contrition.

Thy loving kindness, O Lord, increases my shame and sorrow for having offended Thee. I have sinned against the best of Fathers, the most amiable of Friends,—the Saviour of my soul. I have sinned against Thee; and, instead of punishing me as I deserve, Thou dost spread Thine arms from the cross, to welcome me to Thine embraces, to press me to Thy heart, and to wash me in the sacred blood which issues from it. Thou givest Thyself to me. O my Jesus,—I ought to expire with grief, at the foot of Thy cross. May I, at least, never cease to mingle my tears with the blood Thou hast shed for me.

Let us go and die with Him.—John ch. 11.

Wash me yet more from mine iniquity.—Ps. 50.

An Act of Hope.

In the merits of this sacred blood I put all my confidence. It is the blood of the Lamb Who taketh away the sins of the world. It will take away mine, and I shall obtain mercy. Encouraged by this blessed hope, I present myself before Thine altar, O Jesus, as before the throne of grace. Behold then, O Lord, my weakness, my blindness, and my misery.— Strengthen me, enlighten me, and open to me the treasure of Thy blessings.

In Thee, O Lord, have I hoped, I shall not be confounded forever.—Psalm 30.

The Lord is my Shepherd, I shall want nothing. —Psalm 22.

An Act of Desire and Love.

Thou knockest at the door of my heart, mine amiable Redeemer.—I hear Thy voice, and open to Thee with eagerness and joy. Come, and take possession of this poor heart of mine. Make it Thy dwelling forever. Inflame it with the fire of Thy divine charity. Come my beloved ; come, Lamb of God,—adorable Flesh, precious Blood of my Saviour ;—Come and be the nourishment of my hungry soul. Let me seek Thee, and love Thee alone, O God of my heart ;—my comfort,—my treasure,—my joy,— my life,—my God, and mine all.

Who will give us of His flesh, that we may be satisfied.—Job ch. 31.

As the hart panteth after the fountains of waters, so my soul panteth after Thee, O Lord.—Ps. 44.

When just about to receive, recollect yourself for a few minutes ;

Rejoice, thy King is coming to thee.—Matt. ch. 21.
Behold, the Bridegroom cometh ; go ye forth to meet Him.—Matt. ch. 25.

Observe the words pronounced by the Priest :

"*Corpus Domini nostri Jesu Christi custodiat animam tuam in vitam æternam, Amen*" :—
(May the body of Our Lord Jesus Christ preserve thy soul to life everlasting, Amen) :—for they imply that the end proposed in communicating is not simply to maintain a certain regularity of conduct for a few days, weeks or months ; but to persevere faithfully, to the very moment of death, in that state of grace to which a worthy reception of this divine sacrament shall now raise you.

Prayers After Communion.

Immediately after Communion, bless and adore in silence your Divine Saviour, now residing in your breast : speak to Him as a friend to his friend :—and when, in order to fix your attention, you need any help, recite or meditate on the following prayers :—

An Act of Adoration.

O Divine Jesus, incomprehensible Majesty, before Whom the powers of heaven tremble, Thou art now present in my breast. I bow down before Thee with the most profound sentiments of adoration, astonishment, fear, joy and gratitude. I prostrate myself at Thy feet, like Magdalene :—I offer Thee the homages and adorations of all Thy Saints and Angels in heaven, to supply the defects of mine. O teach me to welcome Thee as I ought.

Thou art my Lord and my God.—John ch. 20.

Hosanna to the Son of David. Blessed is He Who cometh in the name of the Lord. Hosanna in the highest.—Matt. ch. 21.

Thou only art Holy,—Thou only art the Lord,—Thou only art the Most High, O Jesus Christ.—Canticle, Gloria in excelsis, at Mass.

An Act of Love.

My Beloved is mine, and I am His. Jesus, the amiable Jesus, is mine. O may I love Thee, O Lord, as much as Thou hast loved me.—Saints of heaven, Angels of God, Mother of Jesus, lend me your hearts, that, like you, I may burn with the love of Jesus. Yes, O my God, I love Thee with my whole heart and soul; I love Thee above all things. Grant that I may daily increase in Thy love.

I will love Thee, O Lord, my strength. Psalm 17.

O Lord, Thou knowest that I love Thee. John ch. 21.

An Act of Thanksgiving.

O the best of Benefactors :—not content with having died for me on a cross, Thou hast this day bestowed on me Thy sacred flesh and blood, for the nourishment of my soul, the remedy of mine infirmities, the pledge of mine eternal salvation. What thanks shall I return to Thee? Bless the Lord, O my soul, and let all that is within me bless His holy name. Bless the Lord, O my soul, and never forget His incomprehensible favour.—

What shall I render to the Lord.—Psalm 115.
I will bless the Lord at all times:—His praise shall be always in my mouth.—Psalm 33.

An Act of Petition.

Thou comest to me, O Divine spouse of my soul, with a heart overflowing with tenderness, ready to pour upon me Thy choicest favours.— O then do to me, not according to mine unworthiness, but according to the infinite riches of Thy power and liberality. Grant me all the graces which Thou knowest to be necessary to me. Purify my body, sanctify my soul. Take away from my heart whatever displeases Thee. Apply to me the precious merits of Thy life and death. Unite me indissolubly to Thee. Live in me, that I may live in Thee, and for Thee alone. Grant me, in particular, *(here pray for that virtue, or for the victory over that vice or passion, which you most need to acquire or to overcome).* Pour, likewise, Thine abundant blessings over all those, for whom I am bound to pray,— particularly *N. and N.* Grant perseverance to the just, conversion to sinners, eternal peace and refreshment to the faithful departed. Canst

Thou refuse me anything, after Thou hast given me Thyself ?

I shall not let Thee go, till Thou bless me.—Genesis 33.

Do to Thy servant according to Thy great mercy. Psalm 118.

An Act of Oblation.

It is Thy will, O adorable Saviour, that, in return for the gift Thou hast made to me, I should be Thine, and live for Thee alone. It is also my desire, and my firm resolution. To Thee I give my heart, to Thee I consecrate my whole self. Thou shalt be henceforth the sole object of my love, and of all mine affections.— Whatever I have of strength, of power, of health and life ; my body with all its senses ; my soul with all its faculties ; my thoughts, desires, words and actions ; every moment of my life, shall be dedicated to Thy service and glory. Do not reject the poor offering of Thy servant ; do not abandon me to mine enemies.—

I am Thy servant, and the son of Thy handmaid.—Psalm 115.

Into Thy hands, O Lord, I commend my spirit. —Psalm 30.

Firm Purpose of Amendment.

What, O Lord, would be my wickedness and ingratitude, were I ever to disobey Thy holy commandments.—No, my Saviour, I will rather die, than wilfully commit any sin. I renounce forever, pride, impatience, profane discourse, quarrels, animosities, jealousies, covetousness, intemperance, sensuality, sloth, impurity, selfishness, and whatever else can offend Thee. I firmly resolve to live in holiness and righteousness, all the days of my life. It is in Thy presence, Divine Saviour, that I take these resolutions. O grant me grace to be faithful to them ; grant that the word which Thou hast said may be fulfilled in me, *he that eateth Me, the same also shall live by Me.*—John ch. 6.

I have sworn and am determined to keep the judgments of Thy justice.—Psalm 118.

Confirm, O God, what Thou hast wrought in us. —Psalm 67.

I have found Him whom my soul loveth, and I will not let Him go.—Cant. 5.

N.B.—Never leave the Church immediately after having received, but spend sometime in giving thanks :—try also to employ some part of the afternoon in the above or similar exercises of devotion :—and be particularly watchful over yourself during the whole day.

FINIS.

INDEX.

	PAGE
Historical Sketch	iii
Organization of Conferences in Toronto	vii
Do throughout the Province	viii-xiv
Order of Conference Meetings	xvi
Explanations concerning Indulgences	1
Indulgences granted to the Members of the Society, to its Benefactors and to the poor	5
Introduction	11
Rules of the Society	15
General Regulations	31
Organization of the Conferences	32
Order of Meetings	35
Particular Councils	39
General Councils	41
General Meetings	43
Different Members of the Society	44
Feasts of the Society	45
General Observations	46
Instructions to be followed in forming Conferences	49
Instructions on the Duties of Presidents and Vice-Presidents of Councils and Conferences	62
Conditions in the choice of a President	63
Duties of a President in entering on his functions	64

Duties of a President at the Meetings of his Conference	65
Duties of Presidents in regard to the Conference or the Council	68
Particular Duties of Presidents of Conferences	71
Special Duties of Presidents of Councils	76
Duties of a President towards Members	78
Duties with regard to the Clergy	85
Duties of Presidents with regard to the Civil Authorities	88
Duties of Presidents with regard to other Charitable Societies	91
Duties of Presidents towards the Public	93
Personal Duties of a President	96
Prayers at the beginning and end of the Meetings	100
Superior Council of Canada	107
An Easy Method of attending Holy Mass with Profit	112
Mass of the Feast of the Immaculate Conception of the B. V. Mary	11.
Proper Mass of St. Vincent of Paul	12:
Litany of St. Vincent of Paul	125
Another Litany of St. Vincent of Paul	28
Devotions for Communion	133

Revised and approved by the Particular Council of Toronto.

Address Box 287 Post Office, Toronto.

www.ingramcontent.com/pod-product-compliance
Lightning Source LLC
Chambersburg PA
CBHW030317170426
43202CB00009B/1042